HULK™

OFFICIAL STRATEGY GUIDE

By Tim Bogenn

GAME BASICS

MAIN MENU

From the Main Menu you can access Story Mode, Challenge Mode, Options, and Special Features.

STORY MODE MENU

Select New Game to begin Story Mode. You can choose the difficulty level (Easy, Medium, or Hard), but no matter which you chose, once the game is completed the outcome is the same. The type and the amount of enemies encountered are the difference in different difficulty settings.

CRUSH

THIS GUIDE IS WRITTEN WITH THE DIFFICULTY SET TO MEDIUM.

There are 21 levels in Story Mode. Complete Story Mode and save your "complete" save data to unlock the Continue option that appears on the Story Mode menu. The Continue option allows you to replay any of the 21 missions in Story Mode by scrolling through the level list and selecting the desired mission.

CHALLENGE MODE

Certain levels must be completed before you can play any Challenge Mode games. These unlocking procedures are found in the "Challenge Mode" and "Secrets" section of this guide. There are five games to play in Challenge Mode and details and tips on each of these games can be found in the "Challenge Mode" section in this guide.

OPTIONS

Use the Options Menu when you need to input codes, load or save your progress, try new controller configurations, or to view your Challenge Mode scores. Once you've input a code by entering the Code Input option, you must back out and enter the Special Features menu from the Main Menu to activate the code or see what special feature you've unlocked.

SPECIAL FEATURES

The Special Features option on the Main Menu allows you to access Movie Art, Hulk Unleashed, Cheats, and Credits. In the Movie Art screen, only the first option (On The Movie Set) has been unlocked for you, the rest must be unlocked via Universal Unlock Codes. Hulk Unleashed includes trailers from the movie and the making of the game, these are unlocked from the start of the game. Hulk Movie F/X is unlocked via Universal Unlock Code, but the Game Movies can be seen as you unlock them through Story Mode. Finally, the Cheats option is where you enter turn on or off cheats that have been unlocked using codes input through the Options menu or codes that have been input through the Universal Code Input terminals in the game.

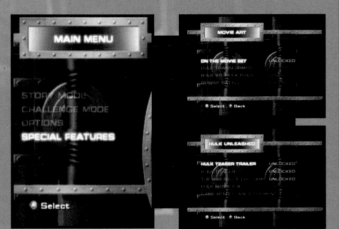

THE CONTROLLER

PLAYSTATION®2 CONTROLS

- GAMMA
- ACTION
- TARGET
- JUMP/CROUCH
- PUNCH
- FREE LOOK
- CHANGE TARGET
- MOVEMENT

GAMECUBE™ CONTROLS

- GAMMA
- ACTION
- TARGET
- JUMP/CROUCH
- PUNCH
- FREE LOOK
- CHANGE TARGET
- MOVEMENT

XBOX™ CONTROLS

- GAMMA
- ACTION
- PUNCH
- TARGET
- JUMP/CROUCH
- FREE LOOK
- CHANGE TARGET
- MOVEMENT

The Hulk has access to a variety of moves, and the moves available to him depend on if he's on the ground, in the air, if he's enraged, or if he is holding an item (or an enemy!). Many moves may be charged, and these moves are marked with a yellow header on a black bar, with a red backdrop. The Hulk is vulnerable while charging any attack.

CRUSH

ALL, NONE OR SOME

IF A CHARGEABLE MOVE IS PART OF A CHAIN, THEN THAT MOVE MAY BE CHARGED SLIGHTLY (MAX CHARGED MOVES HAVE NO FOLLOW UP ATTACKS) AND STILL ALLOW THE CHAIN TO CONTINUE.

FOR EXAMPLE, IN THE LEFT HOOK, RIGHT HOOK, BACKHAND STRING OF ATTACKS, ANY COMBINATION OF THE ATTACKS, FROM ALL TO NONE, COULD BE CHARGED. THE SAME HOLDS TRUE FOR A CHAIN THAT INCLUDES BOTH MOVES THAT CAN'T BE CHARGED AND MOVES THAT CAN. IN THIS CASE, THE LEFT HOOK AND RIGHT HOOK THAT LEAD INTO THE PUNT KICK CAN BOTH BE BRIEFLY CHARGED BEFORE UNLEASHING THE PUNT KICK (WHICH CANNOT BE CHARGED).

GROUND ATTACKS

The following moves are performed when Hulk is in a normal state (not enraged), with his feet on the ground, and not holding any objects or enemies.

LEFT HOOK

PUNCH

LEFT HOOK IS THE BASIC STRIKE IN THE HULK'S ARSENAL. WHEN FULLY CHARGED, THIS MOVE TURNS INTO A HUGE DASHING PUNCH, KNOCKING ENEMIES OUT OF THE WAY AND INFLICTING DOUBLE THE NORMAL DAMAGE.

RIGHT HOOK

PUNCH, PUNCH

ANOTHER BASIC ATTACK, RIGHT HOOK MAY BE CHARGED COMPLETELY TO INFLICT DOUBLE DAMAGE. WHEN FULLY CHARGED, THIS MOVE TURNS INTO A POWERFUL GROUND-SMASH PUNCH THAT BRIEFLY STUNS ALL NEARBY ENEMIES.

BACKHAND

PUNCH, PUNCH, PUNCH

THIS IS A BASIC KNOCKDOWN ATTACK. THE MOVE MAY BE CHARGED FULLY TO INFLICT DOUBLE DAMAGE. WHEN FULLY CHARGED, A WIDE HIT RADIUS THROWS ENEMIES LONG DISTANCES. USE BACKHAND TO KNOCK AWAY MULTIPLE ENEMIES, POTENTIALLY INTO HAZARDS, OR OVER THE SIDES OF BUILDINGS.

GUT PUNCH

(PAUSE AFTER LEFT HOOK OR RIGHT HOOK), PUNCH

GUT PUNCH IS A LEFT (OR LEFT, RIGHT), PAUSE, LEFT PUNCH USED AS A CHANGE OF PACE FROM THE BACKHAND AND TO INITIATE A LONGER COMBO STRING.

RIGHT JAB

(PAUSE AFTER LEFT HOOK OR RIGHT HOOK) PUNCH, PUNCH

RIGHT JAB ISN'T AN ATTACK TO INDUCE NIGHTMARES IN OPPONENTS, BUT IT IS PART OF A LONG COMBO THAT ENDS WITH AN OVERHEAD SMASH.

OVERHEAD SMASH

(PAUSE AFTER LEFT HOOK OR RIGHT HOOK) PUNCH, PUNCH, PUNCH

THIS IS THE FINISHING MOVE TO THE LONGER COMBO. THE SHOCKWAVES ARE GREAT FOR KNOCKING AWAY A GROUP OF ENEMIES.

SHOCKWAVE SLAM

PUNCH + GAMMA

THIS ATTACK SHAKES THE GROUND, DAMAGING ENEMIES INSIDE THE SHOCKWAVES THAT APPEAR AROUND THE HULK. THIS IS A GOOD MOVE TO USE WHEN SURROUNDED. HOWEVER, THE LONG RECOVERY MAKES THE MOVE RISKY IN AREAS WITH PROJECTILE-TOTING ENEMIES.

SONIC CLAP

GAMMA

SONIC CLAP INDUCES A BRIEF STUN IN ENEMIES THAT SHOULD BE USED TO SET UP WITH A MORE DAMAGING ATTACK. THE ENEMIES AFFECTED BY A SONIC CLAP ARE EASY TO SPOT AS THEIR HANDS COVER THEIR EARS. FULLY CHARGED, SONIC CLAP GENERATES A WIDER CONE AND TOSSES SMALL ENEMIES ASIDE. IF HULK'S HANDS STRIKE AN ENEMY, THE STUN IS GREATER. WHEN USED THIS WAY IT CAN EVEN BE USED TO STUN BOSSES! IT HAS A NOTICEABLE RECOVERY TIME, SO DON'T RELY ON THIS MOVE IN CROWDED ROOMS (CROWDED HALLWAYS ARE A DIFFERENT STORY).

2-HANDED UPPER

PUNCH, GAMMA

THIS TECHNIQUE IS GREAT FOR LAUNCHING ENEMIES. PUTTING ENEMIES ON THEIR BACK PROVIDES TIME TO GRAB A WEAPON OR TAKE CARE OF OTHER OPPONENTS.

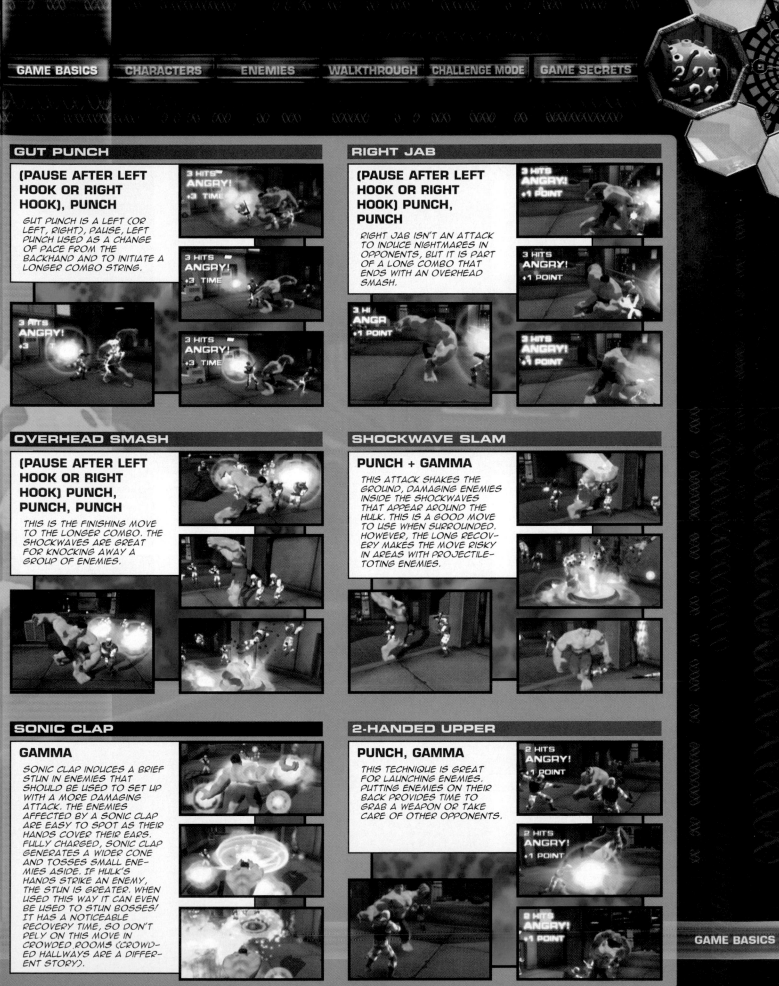

PUNT KICK

PUNCH, PUNCH, GAMMA

THE KICK IS THE IDEAL SETUP FOR A DASH AND SHOULD ALWAYS BE FOLLOWED BY IT UNLESS YOU'RE CONCERNED ABOUT ADEQUATE TIME TO RECOVER.

HAMMER FIST

PUNCH, PUNCH, GAMMA, PUNCH

THIS IS A VERY POWERFUL FINISHER. IT'S EASY TO LEARN AND USE AND IS GREAT AGAINST LARGE OPPONENTS. NOT AS USEFUL AGAINST SMALL ENEMIES WHO WON'T SURVIVE THE KICK.

RISING UPPER

TARGET, BACK, PUNCH

THIS IS A CHARGEABLE 2-HANDED UPPERCUT WITH A SURPRISING AMOUNT OF FORWARD MOVEMENT WHEN RELEASED. MAKE SURE TO BE FACING OPPONENT(S) BEFORE PRESSING THE TARGET BUTTON. THE SOONER THE PUNCH BUTTON IS PRESSED, THE SOONER THE HULK STOPS WALKING BACKWARDS. WHEN PERFORMED QUICKLY ENOUGH, THE HULK WON'T EVEN TAKE A STEP BACK. USE THIS MOVE TO DEFLECT MISSILES OR SEND INCOMING ENEMIES INTO THE AIR.

DASH

FORWARD, FORWARD

HULK LUNGES FORWARD WITH A SHOULDER CHARGE IN THE DIRECTION OF THE DOUBLE-TAP. IT'S A GREAT GENERAL-PURPOSE MOVE FOR PUSHING THROUGH CROWDS, GETTING TROUBLESOME ENEMIES OUT OF THE WAY, DEFLECTING MISSILES OR TO GAIN BREATHING SPACE. THE SLIGHT RECOVERY TIME MAKES IT SOMEWHAT RISKY, SO BE CAREFUL WHERE ANY DASH ENDS. PRACTICE THE DOUBLE TAP UNTIL YOU CAN PERFORM IT ALMOST REFLEXIVELY.

DASHING PUNCH

FORWARD, FORWARD, PUNCH OR TARGET, FORWARD, PUNCH

USE THIS MOVE TO EXTEND DASHES. THIS IS GREAT FOR CLEARING OUT BUNCHED TOGETHER ENEMIES. IT'S MORE DAMAGING THAN A DASH ALONE. THE DOWNSIDE OF THE DASHING PUNCH IS ITS LENGTHY RECOVERY.

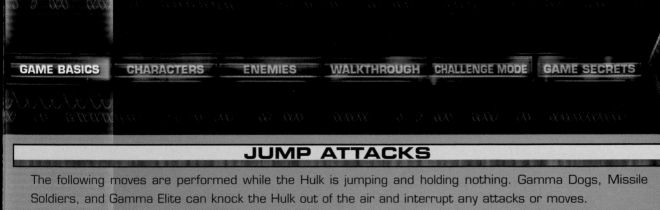
JUMP ATTACKS

The following moves are performed while the Hulk is jumping and holding nothing. Gamma Dogs, Missile Soldiers, and Gamma Elite can knock the Hulk out of the air and interrupt any attacks or moves.

GAMMA CRUSHER

JUMP, PUNCH

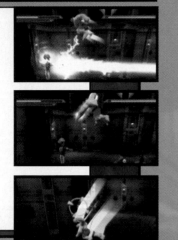

WHILE IN THE AIR, HOLD PUNCH TO CHARGE THE ATTACK. SELECT A TARGET BEFORE JUMPING SO THAT THE HULK FLIES IN THAT DIRECTION. THERE IS A SMALL WINDOW OF TIME WHILE IN THE AIR TO READ-JUST, IF NECESSARY. THE RANGE OF THE JUMP IS LIM-ITED, SO THERE'S NO ASSURANCE OF HITTING A DISTANT TARGET. USE GAMMA CRUSHER TO DODGE AN ATTACK OR PROJECTILE, THEN CHARGE AND CRASH DOWN ON THE RECOVERING ENEMY. THE LONGER THIS MOVE IS CHARGED, THE GREATER ITS RECOVERY TIME.

GAMMA STOMP

JUMP, GAMMA

GAMMA STOMP IS A POWER-FUL TECHNIQUE THAT DROPS DOWN FROM THE POINT WHERE THE GAMMA BUTTON IS PRESSED, MAKING THE SELECTION OF A TARGET LESS NECESSARY. THE LONGER THE MOVE IS CHARGED, THE LARGER THE SHOCKWAVE. A QUICK ATTACK STUNS NEARBY ENE-MIES, WHILE A CHARGED ATTACK SENDS THEM FLYING.

GRAPPLES

A grapple move is one that follows the picking up of an enemy, no matter if the Hulk is enraged or not. These moves do not apply to grabbed objects. Press the Action button when close to pick up an enemy. Smaller enemies and larger enemies act differently. Larger enemies will eventually struggle free—so act quickly! Gamma Dogs are essentially immune to grappling, a Punt Kick is performed instead of picking up one.

TOSS

ACTION

THROW AN ENEMY INTO DAN-GER, AGAINST HAZARDOUS OBJECTS, OR INTO OTHER ENEMIES. RANGE ISN'T AN ISSUE FOR THE HULK, BUT ENVIRONMENTAL OBSTACLES HINDER ACCURACY.

MULTI-STRIKE THROW

PUNCH

WHEN HOLDING A SMALL ENEMY, THE HULK'S SPEED REMAINS THE SAME, AND HE RETAINS THE ABILITY TO JUMP. HOLDING LARGE ENEMIES SLOWS DOWN, AND GROUNDS, THE HULK. WHILE MOST HELD ENEMIES ARE BEST USED AS PROJECTILES (SEE TOSS), OTHER ATTACK OPTIONS EXIST. PRESS PUNCH A FEW TIMES FOR A LEFT, RIGHT HOOK (PUNCH, PUNCH) OR A LEFT, RIGHT HOOK, HEADBUTT (PUNCH, PUNCH, PUNCH).

THERE IS A SHORT AMOUNT OF TIME TO PRESS PUNCH AFTER GRABBING A LARGE OPPONENT, AS THEY TRY TO STRUGGLE FREE. A SHORT ANIMATION ILLUSTRATES A SPECIAL MOVE, AND DURING THIS ANIMATION THE HULK IS INVULNERABLE (MISSILES DO NO DAMAGE, NO ENEMIES CAN GRAB HIM, ETC.). IN THIS TIME, IT'S POSSIBLE TO TARGET ANOTHER OPPONENT AND SLAM THE HELD ENEMY INTO THE TAR-GET (THIS IS DIFFERENT FROM A TOSS). BE CAREFUL WHEN AIMING THE SLAM; THE HULK IS VULNERABLE TO ATTACK WHEN ENEMIES ARE LIFTED OVER HIS HEAD. KEEP PUNCH PRESSED TO GET THE SECOND SLAM.

GAMMA SLAM

GAMMA

THIS POWERFUL SLAM FINISHES OFF ANYONE BUT THE HARDIEST OF OPPONENTS. LARGE ENEMIES ARE RUN THROUGH A HANDFUL OF PROFESSIONAL WRESTLING INSPIRED MOVES. OUCH! SMALLER ENEMIES BECOME ONE WITH THE FLOOR. DOUBLE OUCH!

JUMPING THROW

JUMP, ACTION

THIS WORKS ONLY WITH SMALL ENEMIES. USE THE TARGET BUTTON TO THROW THE ENEMY AT A SPECIFIC TARGET.

HULK POWER-UPS

There are three kinds of power-up: Health, Rage, and Continue. Continues are usually found hidden behind or inside objects. Health and Rage power-ups commonly appear over the bodies of defeated enemies and destroyed environmental objects. Smash everything in every area to find all that the level has to offer.

CONTINUE

WHEN THE HEALTH METER COMPLETELY EMPTIES, YOU ARE PROMPTED TO RETRY, QUIT, OR CONTINUE. RETRY TAKES YOU BACK TO THE BEGINNING OF THE LEVEL, BUT DOES NOT USE UP A CONTINUE. CONTINUE TAKES YOU BACK TO THE LAST CHECKPOINT PASSED. THESE ARE USUALLY AREAS THAT BEGIN WITH A CINEMATIC AND MAY BE AS INSIGNIFICANT AS A BREAKING DOWN A DOOR. THE STORY MODE INITIALLY PROVIDES THREE CONTINUES, THE REST MUST BE COLLECTED THROUGHOUT THE ADVENTURE.

HEALTH

THESE GREEN SPHERES ADD TO THE HEALTH METER USED BY BOTH BRUCE BANNER AND THE HULK. THEY COME IN TWO SIZES, MAJOR AND MINOR. OBJECTS THAT HOLD HEALTH POWER-UPS USUALLY REGENERATE, AND MOST OF THE TIME, THE POWER-UP REGENERATES WITH THE OBJECT.

RAGE

RAGE POWER-UPS ALSO COME IN TWO SIZES, MAJOR AND MINOR. COLLECTED RAGE ICONS ADD TO THE RAGE METER, WHICH IS ONLY USED BY THE HULK. WHEN THE RAGE METER FILLS, THE HULK ENTERS RAGE MODE WHERE DAMAGE IS DOUBLED AND SPECIAL RAGE MOVES BECOME AVAILABLE.

CRUSH

NATURAL RAGE

HITTING AND DEFEATING OPPONENTS ADDS TO THE RAGE METER. THE BETTER THE COMBO THE MORE RAGE ADDED.

RAGE ATTACKS

The following attacks can only be performed when the Rage Meter has filled, and the Hulk's hands are free. Using these moves completely drains the Rage Meter. The Hulk is invulnerable while performing these attacks.

SMASH

IT'S ALL THE RAGE!

WHEN HULK IS IN RAGE MODE, ALL DAMAGE IS DOUBLED. THERE'S NO REASON TO CHARGE THE SONIC CLAP AS EACH CLAP IS ALWAYS FULLY CHARGED. THE BEST STRATEGY IS TO DAMAGE ENEMIES USING REGULAR ATTACKS WHILE THE RAGE METER DWINDLES, THEN AS THE METER IS ABOUT TO EMPTY, TRIGGER EITHER THE SUPER SONIC CLAP OR SUPER OVERHAND SMASH.

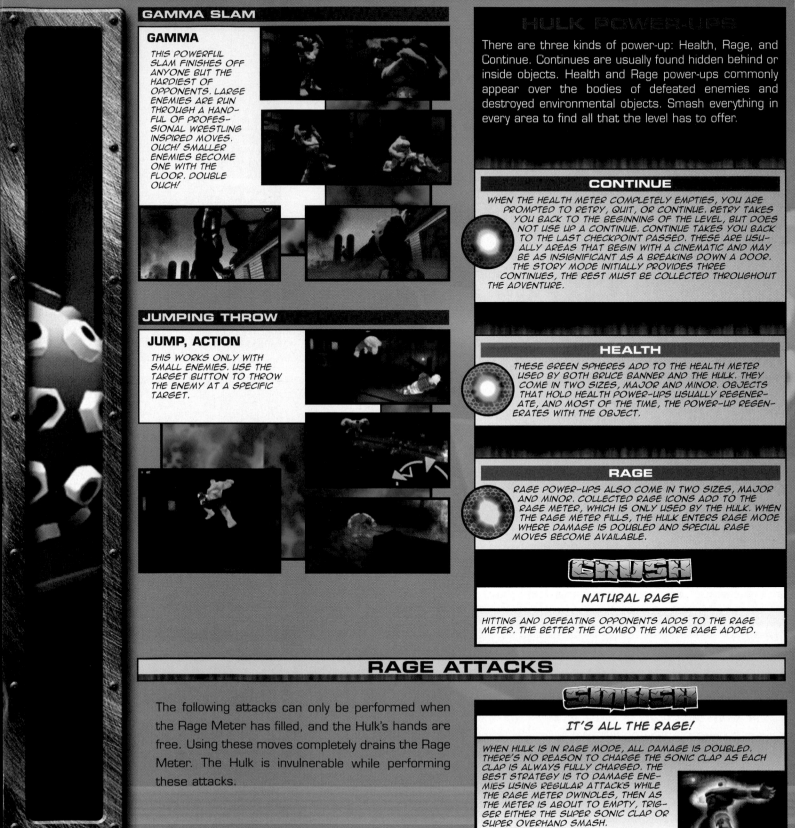

SUPER SONIC CLAP

GAMMA + ACTION

SUPER SONIC CLAP IS HULK'S MOST POWERFUL TECHNIQUE. IT SENDS OUT A HUGE WAVE, CAUSING MASSIVE DAMAGE TO ANYONE AND ANYTHING IT HITS. THIS ALSO CREATES A SHOCKWAVE AROUND THE HULK, FLOORING ANY NEARBY ENEMIES. FLOORING ENEMIES BEFORE PERFORMING HELPS WITH ACCURACY, ESPECIALLY AGAINST BOSSES.

SUPER OVERHAND SMASH

PUNCH + GAMMA

SUPER OVERHAND SMASH CAUSES A HUGE SHOCKWAVE OF DAMAGE AROUND HULK, INFLICTING EXTREME DAMAGE TO EVERYONE, AND EVERYTHING NEARBY. THIS TECHNIQUE IS NOT AS POWERFUL AS THE SUPER SONIC CLAP AND HAS A SHORTER RANGE, BUT IS SAFER TO USE, AS IT'S NEARLY IMPOSSIBLE TO ESCAPE AND DOES NOT HAVE TO BE AIMED.

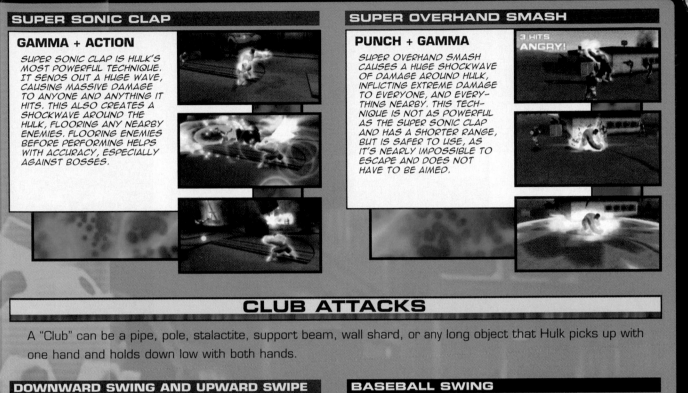

CLUB ATTACKS

A "Club" can be a pipe, pole, stalactite, support beam, wall shard, or any long object that Hulk picks up with one hand and holds down low with both hands.

DOWNWARD SWING AND UPWARD SWIPE

PUNCH OR PUNCH, PUNCH

PRESS PUNCH ONCE TO GET ONE DOWNWARD SWING, PRESSING PUNCH TWICE RESULTS IN TWO SWINGS, ONE DOWNWARD, FOLLOWED BY AN UPWARD SWIPE.

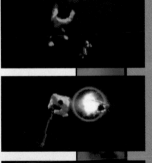

BASEBALL SWING

PUNCH, PUNCH, GAMMA

PERFORM AN UPWARD SWIPE, THEN HOLD THE GAMMA BUTTON AND IT'S "TAKE ME OUT TO THE BALLPARK" TIME. BASEBALL SWING KNOCKS ENEMIES OFF LEDGES, INTO HAZARDOUS OBJECTS, OR INTO EACH OTHER. MAKE A HABIT OF LEARNING THIS MOVE EARLY, THEN WORK ON USING IT OFTEN.

BATTERING RAM

TARGET, FORWARD, PUNCH

THIS IS USEFUL FOR A QUICK KNOCKDOWN AND SQUISHING MISSILE SOLDIERS THAT HIDE IN TIGHT CORNERS. IT'S FASTER THAN THE OVERHEAD SMASH, BUT NOT AS EFFECTIVE.

OVERHEAD SMASH

GAMMA

OVERHEAD SMASH IS A SINGLE, POWERFUL ATTACK THAT CREATES A SHOCKWAVE WHEN THE CLUB HITS THE GROUND. USEFUL FOR TAKING OUT SINGLE LARGE ENEMIES OR QUICKLY FLOORING A TIGHTLY PACKED GROUP OF SMALLER ENEMIES. IT HAPPENS TO BE THE BEST DAMAGE OF ALL THE SINGLE HITS.

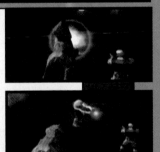
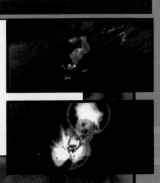

GAME BASICS

Heavy objects are items that the Hulk picks up with both hands and holds over his head. When wielding objects as the Hulk, pay close attention to the shape of the object. Its shape determines the strike area for each attack, smash or swing. Discover which objects are most effective with each attack. There shouldn't be a problem finding eager test subjects.

THROW OBJECT

ACTION

SOME OBJECTS CAN BE TOSSED, PICKED UP AND THROWN REPEATEDLY. THROWING AN OBJECT DOES NOT HARM THE HULK, NO MATTER HOW CLOSE HE IS TO THE EXPLOSION.

SMASH

PUNCH

SMASH IS THE SINGLE MOST POWERFUL TECHNIQUE WITH A WEAPON. THIS DRIVES THE OBJECT DOWN, CRUSHING ENEMIES INTO THE GROUND. THE LARGER THE OBJECT, THE MORE DAMAGE DONE, AND THE LARGER THE STRIKE AREA. SOME OBJECTS EXPLODE (BARRELS, GAS TANKS ETC.) AND CAUSE MORE DAMAGE THAN THE OBJECT ITSELF.

SWING

GAMMA

THIS MOVE CAUSES HULK TO SWIPE THE OBJECT FROM HIS EXTREME RIGHT TO HIS EXTREME LEFT. SWINGING AN OBJECT IS GREAT FOR TAKING OUT A LARGE GROUP OF SURROUNDING ENEMIES, BUT IT'S NOT AS DAMAGING AS SMASH. IT'S MOST USEFUL AGAINST GROUPS OF ENEMIES OR FAST-MOVING ATTACKERS.

BRUCE BANNER'S MOVES

There are many levels that involve the emotionally disturbed scientist, Bruce Banner. Bruce can fight, but nothing like his inner beast. His resistance to beatings is low and if he becomes angry, you could fail the mission.

BASIC PUNCHES

PUNCH

BANNER HAS A BASIC 3-PUNCH COMBO, WHICH KNOCKS DOWN ANY OTHER HUMAN. A 2-HIT COMBO INTO A GRAB INFLICTS THE MOST DAMAGE. WHEN FACING ONLY ONE ENEMY, THE BEST STRATEGY IS TO REPEATEDLY PERFORM THE FIRST TWO STRIKES OF THE COMBO, AND OVERCOME HIM WITHOUT GOING INTO THE KNOCKDOWN.

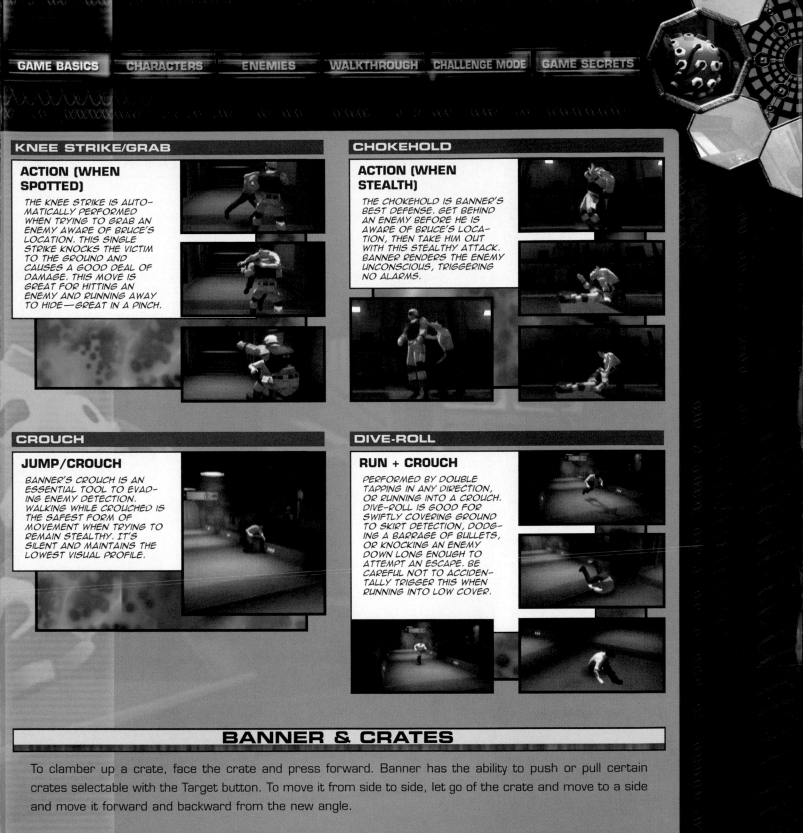

KNEE STRIKE/GRAB

ACTION (WHEN SPOTTED)

THE KNEE STRIKE IS AUTOMATICALLY PERFORMED WHEN TRYING TO GRAB AN ENEMY AWARE OF BRUCE'S LOCATION. THIS SINGLE STRIKE KNOCKS THE VICTIM TO THE GROUND AND CAUSES A GOOD DEAL OF DAMAGE. THIS MOVE IS GREAT FOR HITTING AN ENEMY AND RUNNING AWAY TO HIDE—GREAT IN A PINCH.

CHOKEHOLD

ACTION (WHEN STEALTH)

THE CHOKEHOLD IS BANNER'S BEST DEFENSE. GET BEHIND AN ENEMY BEFORE HE IS AWARE OF BRUCE'S LOCATION, THEN TAKE HIM OUT WITH THIS STEALTHY ATTACK. BANNER RENDERS THE ENEMY UNCONSCIOUS, TRIGGERING NO ALARMS.

CROUCH

JUMP/CROUCH

BANNER'S CROUCH IS AN ESSENTIAL TOOL TO EVADING ENEMY DETECTION. WALKING WHILE CROUCHED IS THE SAFEST FORM OF MOVEMENT WHEN TRYING TO REMAIN STEALTHY. IT'S SILENT AND MAINTAINS THE LOWEST VISUAL PROFILE.

DIVE-ROLL

RUN + CROUCH

PERFORMED BY DOUBLE TAPPING IN ANY DIRECTION, OR RUNNING INTO A CROUCH. DIVE-ROLL IS GOOD FOR SWIFTLY COVERING GROUND TO SKIRT DETECTION, DODGING A BARRAGE OF BULLETS, OR KNOCKING AN ENEMY DOWN LONG ENOUGH TO ATTEMPT AN ESCAPE. BE CAREFUL NOT TO ACCIDENTALLY TRIGGER THIS WHEN RUNNING INTO LOW COVER.

BANNER & CRATES

To clamber up a crate, face the crate and press forward. Banner has the ability to push or pull certain crates selectable with the Target button. To move it from side to side, let go of the crate and move to a side and move it forward and backward from the new angle.

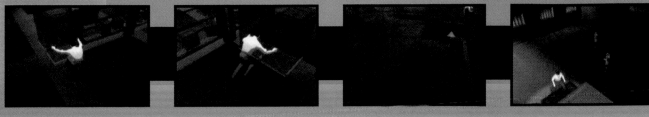

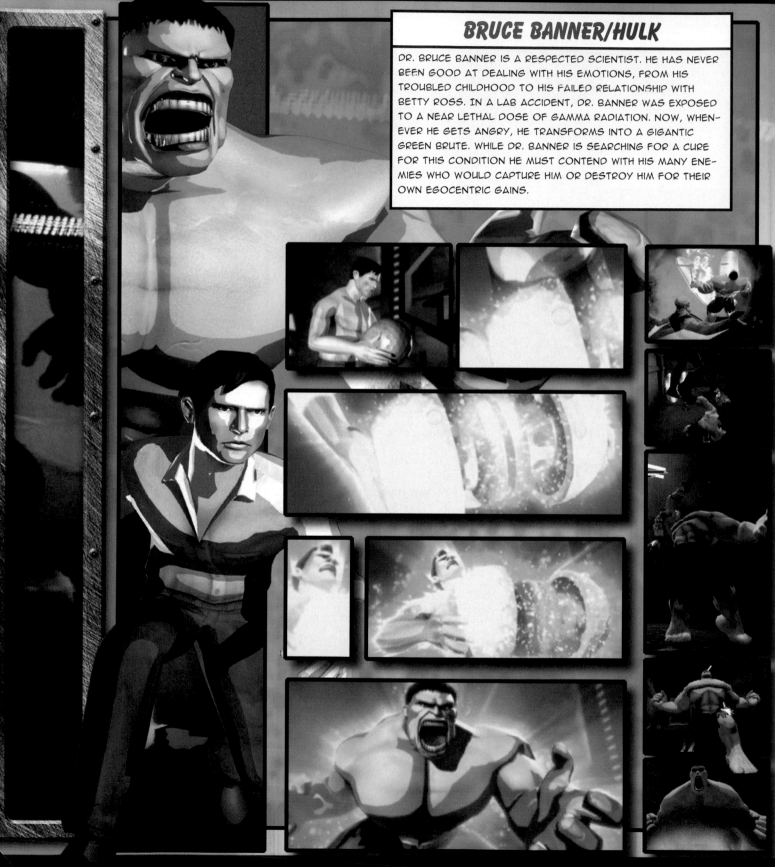

BRUCE BANNER/HULK

DR. BRUCE BANNER IS A RESPECTED SCIENTIST. HE HAS NEVER BEEN GOOD AT DEALING WITH HIS EMOTIONS, FROM HIS TROUBLED CHILDHOOD TO HIS FAILED RELATIONSHIP WITH BETTY ROSS. IN A LAB ACCIDENT, DR. BANNER WAS EXPOSED TO A NEAR LETHAL DOSE OF GAMMA RADIATION. NOW, WHEN-EVER HE GETS ANGRY, HE TRANSFORMS INTO A GIGANTIC GREEN BRUTE. WHILE DR. BANNER IS SEARCHING FOR A CURE FOR THIS CONDITION HE MUST CONTEND WITH HIS MANY ENE-MIES WHO WOULD CAPTURE HIM OR DESTROY HIM FOR THEIR OWN EGOCENTRIC GAINS.

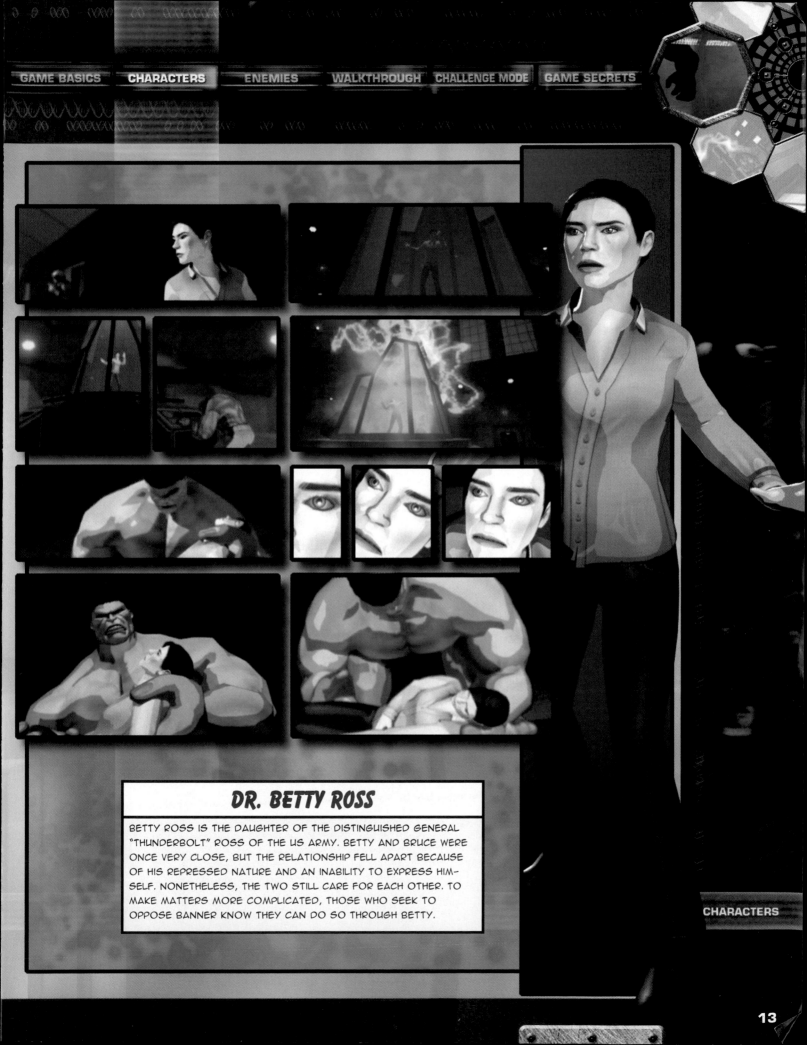

DR. BETTY ROSS

BETTY ROSS IS THE DAUGHTER OF THE DISTINGUISHED GENERAL "THUNDERBOLT" ROSS OF THE US ARMY. BETTY AND BRUCE WERE ONCE VERY CLOSE, BUT THE RELATIONSHIP FELL APART BECAUSE OF HIS REPRESSED NATURE AND AN INABILITY TO EXPRESS HIMSELF. NONETHELESS, THE TWO STILL CARE FOR EACH OTHER. TO MAKE MATTERS MORE COMPLICATED, THOSE WHO SEEK TO OPPOSE BANNER KNOW THEY CAN DO SO THROUGH BETTY.

CHARACTERS

PROFESSOR CRAWFORD/RAVAGE

PROFESSOR CRAWFORD IS A BRILLIANT SCIENTIST AND RESEARCHER, AND BRUCE BANNER WAS HIS GREATEST STUDENT. CRAWFORD IS NOW A SICKLY MAN, LIVING OUT HIS TWILIGHT YEARS FROM THE CONFINES OF A WHEELCHAIR. EMBITTERED BY HIS CONDITION, PROFESSOR CRAWFORD IS OBSESSED WITH REGAINING HIS HEALTH AT ANY COST. HE HAS FOUND THAT USING GAMMA POWER HE CAN TURN INTO A FORM HE CALLS "RAVAGE," A HULK-LIKE MONSTER. IN RAVAGE FORM HE EXHIBITS HULK-CLASS STRENGTH AND SIMILAR ABILITIES.

THE GAMMA ORB IS PROFESSOR CRAWFORD'S ADAPTATION OF BANNER'S OWN GAMMA-POWER RESEARCH. CRAWFORD HAS REVERSE-ENGINEERED BANNER'S OWN GAMMASPHERE IN AN ATTEMPT TO CREATE A NEW, MORE COMPACT DUAL-FUNCTION DEVICE. THE GAMMA ORB IS CAPABLE OF ABSORBING AND STORING VAST QUANTITIES OF ENERGY FROM ANY SOURCE IN CLOSE PROXIMITY. ADDITIONALLY, IT CAN EMIT THOSE STORED ENERGIES IN AN ATTEMPT TO INDUCE LOW-LEVEL CELLULAR STRUCTURE CHANGES IN SUBJECTS BY MANIPULATING CELLULAR DISTRESS SIGNALS. ANYONE SURVIVING THIS PROCESS WOULD BE CLASSIFIED AS A MUTANT WITH ENHANCED CLASS 10 TISSUE, AND SUBSTANTIALLY MORE PHYSICAL MASS.

THE GAMMA ORB

ENEMIES

THERE ARE TWO FACTIONS ENGAGED IN HUNTING THE HULK, THE MILITARY, AND THE LEADER'S FORCES. THE HULK FACES GENERAL RYKER'S MILITARY IN CHAPTERS 1 AND 3. THE LEADERS FORCES HARRASS THE HULK IN CHAPTERS 2, 4 AND 5.

THE GENERAL'S FORCES

THE MILITARY WEARS DESERT UNIFORMS AND RESEMBLE THE US ARMED FORCES OF TODAY. THESE SOLDIERS ARE STATIONED AT GAMMA BASE AND HUNT BOTH BANNER AND THE HULK UNDER GENERAL RYKER'S ORDERS.

RIFLE SOLDIERS

EQUIPPED WITH AN M-16 AND DRESSED IN DESERT UNIFORMS, THE RIFLE SOLDIERS ARE THE RANK AND FILE IN RYKER'S MILITARY UNITS.

MISSILE SOLDIERS

EQUIPPED WITH THE JAVELIN MISSILE SYSTEM, MISSILE SOLDIERS MAKE YOU THINK TWICE ABOUT JUMPING IN THE AIR. THESE SOLDIERS ARE OFTEN THE BIGGEST THREAT IN THE FIELD.

SHOCK TROOPERS

EQUIPPED WITH ELECTRIFIED STUN BATONS, THE SHOCK TROOPERS STICK TOGETHER AND FIGHT AS A CLOSE-COMBAT TROOP.

SHOCKSHIELDERS

EQUIPPED WITH ELECTRIFIED STUN BATONS AND PORTABLE PLASMA SHIELD GENERATORS, THE SHOCKSHIELDERS ARE IMPENETRABLE AND DEADLY. HOWEVER, WHEN THE SHIELD IS DISENGAGED, THE SOLDIER IS AS VULNERABLE AS THE REST. THROW ENVIRONMENTAL OBJECTS (OTHER ENEMIES BOUNCE OFF THE SHIELD) AT THE SOLDIERS TO POWER DOWN THEIR SHIELDS.

GENERAL RYKER

THE MAN LEADING THE MILITARY FORCES. CLEAN GLOVES HIDE DIRTY HANDS, AND GENERAL RYKER'S HANDS ARE DIRTIER THAN MOST. THE SHADOWY RYKER IS IN CHARGE OF AN UNKNOWN NUMBER OF UNDOCUMENTED BLACK OP UNITS. RUTHLESS AND AMBITIOUS, RYKER IS MORE INTERESTED IN FURTHERING HIS OWN POWER THAN SERVING HIS COUNTRY. WITH THE MILITARY MIGHT AND FAR-SEEING INTELLIGENCE ABILITIES OF THE UNITED STATES ARMED FORCES AT HIS DISPOSAL, GENERAL RYKER HUNTS THE HULK. HIS GOAL IS TO CAPTURE AND STUDY THE HULK, TO UNLOCK THE DANGEROUS POWER OF GAMMA MUTATION AND USE IT FOR HIS OWN ENDS.

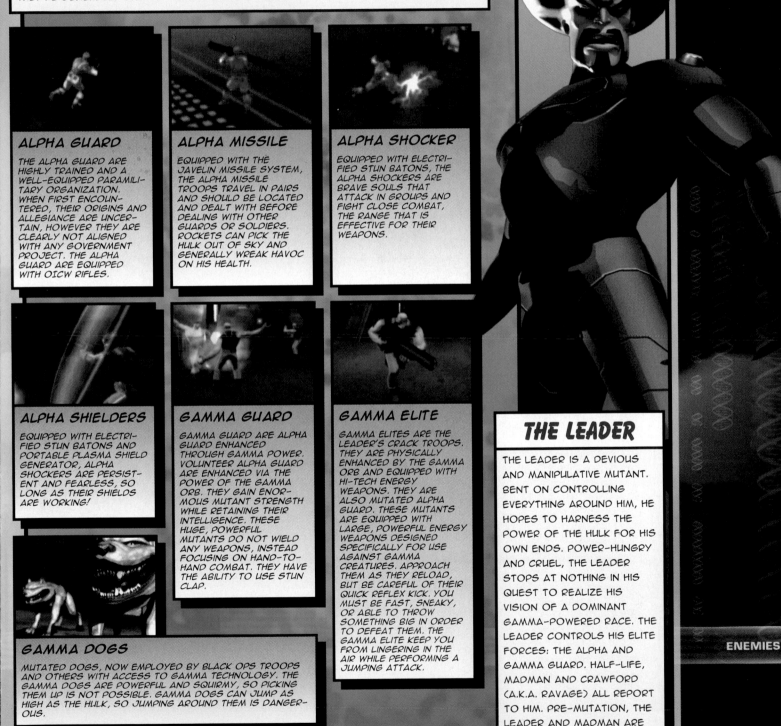

THE LEADER'S FORCES

LEADER'S FORCES ARE A PARAMILITARY OUTFIT CREATED BY THE LEADER HIMSELF AND RESEMBLE A HIGH-TECH COVERT FORCE. THE LEADER'S LOGO IS ON THEIR CLOTHING AND THEY'RE GENERALLY CLAD IN DARK BLUE BODY ARMOR.

ALPHA GUARD

THE ALPHA GUARD ARE HIGHLY TRAINED AND A WELL-EQUIPPED PARAMILI-TARY ORGANIZATION. WHEN FIRST ENCOUN-TERED, THEIR ORIGINS AND ALLEGIANCE ARE UNCER-TAIN, HOWEVER THEY ARE CLEARLY NOT ALIGNED WITH ANY GOVERNMENT PROJECT. THE ALPHA GUARD ARE EQUIPPED WITH OICW RIFLES.

ALPHA MISSILE

EQUIPPED WITH THE JAVELIN MISSILE SYSTEM, THE ALPHA MISSILE TROOPS TRAVEL IN PAIRS AND SHOULD BE LOCATED AND DEALT WITH BEFORE DEALING WITH OTHER GUARDS OR SOLDIERS. ROCKETS CAN PICK THE HULK OUT OF SKY AND GENERALLY WREAK HAVOC ON HIS HEALTH.

ALPHA SHOCKER

EQUIPPED WITH ELECTRI-FIED STUN BATONS, THE ALPHA SHOCKERS ARE BRAVE SOULS THAT ATTACK IN GROUPS AND FIGHT CLOSE COMBAT, THE RANGE THAT IS EFFECTIVE FOR THEIR WEAPONS.

ALPHA SHIELDERS

EQUIPPED WITH ELECTRI-FIED STUN BATONS AND PORTABLE PLASMA SHIELD GENERATOR, ALPHA SHOCKERS ARE PERSIST-ENT AND FEARLESS, SO LONG AS THEIR SHIELDS ARE WORKING!

GAMMA GUARD

GAMMA GUARD ARE ALPHA GUARD ENHANCED THROUGH GAMMA POWER. VOLUNTEER ALPHA GUARD ARE ENHANCED VIA THE POWER OF THE GAMMA ORB. THEY GAIN ENOR-MOUS MUTANT STRENGTH WHILE RETAINING THEIR INTELLIGENCE. THESE HUGE, POWERFUL MUTANTS DO NOT WIELD ANY WEAPONS, INSTEAD FOCUSING ON HAND-TO-HAND COMBAT. THEY HAVE THE ABILITY TO USE STUN CLAP.

GAMMA ELITE

GAMMA ELITES ARE THE LEADER'S CRACK TROOPS. THEY ARE PHYSICALLY ENHANCED BY THE GAMMA ORB AND EQUIPPED WITH HI-TECH ENERGY WEAPONS. THEY ARE ALSO MUTATED ALPHA GUARD. THESE MUTANTS ARE EQUIPPED WITH LARGE, POWERFUL ENERGY WEAPONS DESIGNED SPECIFICALLY FOR USE AGAINST GAMMA CREATURES. APPROACH THEM AS THEY RELOAD, BUT BE CAREFUL OF THEIR QUICK REFLEX KICK. YOU MUST BE FAST, SNEAKY, OR ABLE TO THROW SOMETHING BIG IN ORDER TO DEFEAT THEM. THE GAMMA ELITE KEEP YOU FROM LINGERING IN THE AIR WHILE PERFORMING A JUMPING ATTACK.

GAMMA DOGS

MUTATED DOGS, NOW EMPLOYED BY BLACK OPS TROOPS AND OTHERS WITH ACCESS TO GAMMA TECHNOLOGY. THE GAMMA DOGS ARE POWERFUL AND SQUIRMY, SO PICKING THEM UP IS NOT POSSIBLE. GAMMA DOGS CAN JUMP AS HIGH AS THE HULK, SO JUMPING AROUND THEM IS DANGER-OUS.

THE LEADER

THE LEADER IS A DEVIOUS AND MANIPULATIVE MUTANT. BENT ON CONTROLLING EVERYTHING AROUND HIM, HE HOPES TO HARNESS THE POWER OF THE HULK FOR HIS OWN ENDS. POWER-HUNGRY AND CRUEL, THE LEADER STOPS AT NOTHING IN HIS QUEST TO REALIZE HIS VISION OF A DOMINANT GAMMA-POWERED RACE. THE LEADER CONTROLS HIS ELITE FORCES: THE ALPHA AND GAMMA GUARD. HALF-LIFE, MADMAN AND CRAWFORD (A.K.A. RAVAGE) ALL REPORT TO HIM. PRE-MUTATION, THE LEADER AND MADMAN ARE BIOLOGICAL BROTHERS.

ENEMIES

INNER TORMENT

Bruce Banner endures a life with a troubled recent past, yet filled with dreams. As a genetic scientist, Banner studies the effects of gamma radiation on damaged tissue. Unaware that there is a monster inside him, Banner continually struggles with fits of anxiety, embarrassment and rage. One day during a freak lab accident, Banner's inner beast is unleashed and he becomes the most powerful being on the face of the earth—The Hulk.

KIRBY'S FUELING STATION

CRUSH

MYSTERIOUS PAST

WHEN THE GAME BEGINS, YOU GET THE FEELING OF JUST WALKING INTO THE MIDDLE OF A MOVIE! NOT IN THE SENSE OF STUNNING SPECIAL EFFECTS, SUDDEN ACTION, OR SOME LOSER YELLING AT YOU TO SIT DOWN. INSTEAD, IT'S THE LACK OF EXPLANATION AS TO WHY THIS MAN IS DRIVING IN THE MIDDLE OF THE DESERT AND WHY HE MORPHS INTO A HUGE GREEN BEAST WHEN HE LOOKS INTO A GRIMY BATHROOM MIRROR. THE REASON FOR THIS CONFUSION: THE GAME IS ACTUALLY A CONTINUATION OF THE MOVIE, THE HULK, WHICH IS SET TO RELEASE ABOUT A MONTH AFTER THE GAME. ALTHOUGH SOME LOCATIONS IN THE GAME ARE SIMILAR TO THE MOVIE LOCATIONS, THE STORYLINE PICKS UP WHERE THE MOVIE ENDED.

After the Hulk forces his presence into Bruce's afternoon, he breaks out of Kirby's Fueling Station through the bathroom wall. The military (lead by General Ryker) arrives through a cloud of desert sand and storms the property.

Helpful text messages appear throughout the level offering hints on what buttons to press to perform basic moves. The hints, however, do not explain what moves work best for each situation that arises. The number of soldiers seems over-

whelming at first, but as you progress through the game you begin to welcome these soldiers for the power-ups they leave after you squish them. This level is more or less a training level and you don't have to follow the onscreen prompts. Take advantage of this area and experiment with all of the Hulk's moves and with the objects scattered throughout the area.

SQUASHING TINY SOLDIERS

When attacked by large groups of soldiers, back up to make the advancing crowd bottleneck together. Backing up also gives you time to charge attacks before being interrupted by the angry mob. Face the crowd and perform a Sonic Clap. This attack knocks down all the soldiers it makes contact with and gives you combo bonuses. Combo bonuses add more rage to the Rage Meter than single attacks. One normal Sonic Clap attack does not wipe out the soldiers; however, if enraged this attack is quite deadly.

GROUNDING BOTHERSOME HELICOPTERS

The helicopters carry troops to the fight scene, but offer little other assistance to the battle. Defeating helicopters is not necessary (most of the time) but it's a heck of a good time! Jump up on the roof of Kirby's Fueling Station with a car or dumpster in hand and target one of the helicopters (you may need to toggle between targets). Throw the object at the chopper and watch it go down in flames!

Press ✕ to attack enemies

Press ✕ to attack

CRUSH

WITHIN YOUR GRASP

KIRBY'S GAS STATION IS CHOCK-FULL OF COOL THINGS. ANYTHING THAT CAN BE PICKED UP CAN BE THROWN AT (OR USED TO BEAT UP) THE PUNY HUMANS AND THEIR TOYS OF WAR. LOOK FOR THE FOLLOWING OBJECT TO POUND OR PICK UP AND THROW: LARGE PARKING CURBS, PROPANE TANKS (KNOCK 'EM DOWN THEN PICK 'EM UP), CRATES (LOOK AROUND THE BACK OF THE STATION FOR MORE), LARGE RUSTY PIPE (AROUND BACK), DUMPSTERS, THE LARGE KIRBY'S SIGN (KNOCK IT DOWN AND GRAB THE POLE), AND EXPLODING GAS PUMPS (DESTROY THEM AND MORE DAMAGE IS DONE TO THE ENEMY THAN IS INFLICTED ON YOU).

CRUSHING MEASLY TANKS

When General Ryker orders the tank to the front line, don't sweat it. If you can knock a few rounds back at the tank, the tank goes "Boom!" Face the tank when the round is launched and time the button press to punch the missile back at the tank. Since there is a slight pause between the release of a button and the execution of a move, you must allow for the start-up animation of the punch in order to successfully strike the missile. Make sure that you stand in a position where you can see the flight of the missile. All the tanks in this game have shields that are activated when you are near them. Projectiles, like the tank rounds you knock back at them, do not trigger the tank shield. An alternative for defeating tanks involves picking up large items and either throwing them or using the item to pound the tank.

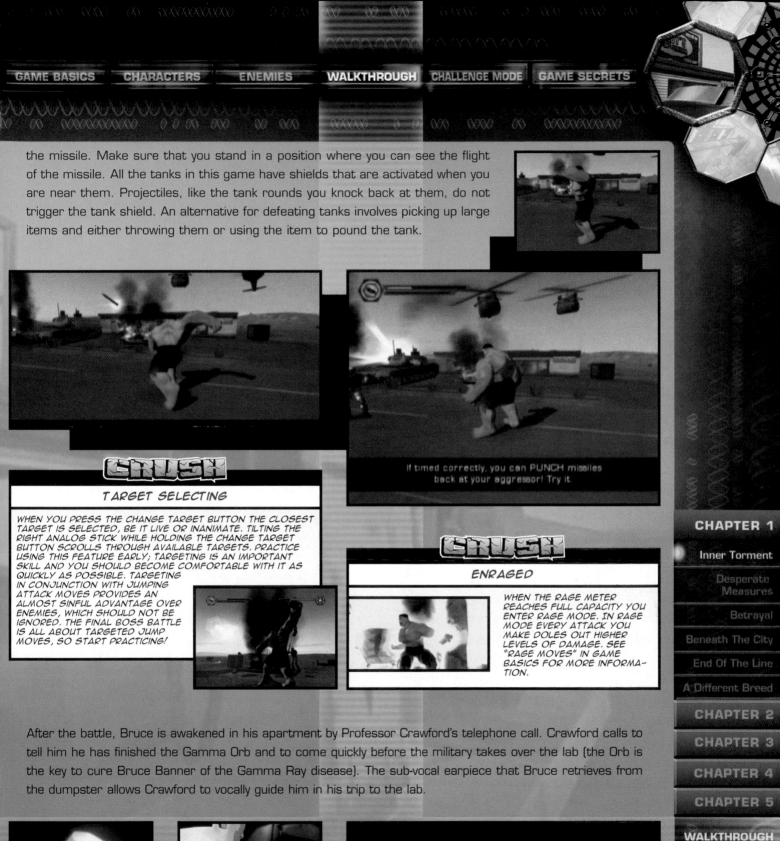

If timed correctly, you can PUNCH missiles back at your aggressor! Try it.

CRUSH

TARGET SELECTING

WHEN YOU PRESS THE CHANGE TARGET BUTTON THE CLOSEST TARGET IS SELECTED, BE IT LIVE OR INANIMATE. TILTING THE RIGHT ANALOG STICK WHILE HOLDING THE CHANGE TARGET BUTTON SCROLLS THROUGH AVAILABLE TARGETS. PRACTICE USING THIS FEATURE EARLY; TARGETING IS AN IMPORTANT SKILL AND YOU SHOULD BECOME COMFORTABLE WITH IT AS QUICKLY AS POSSIBLE. TARGETING IN CONJUNCTION WITH JUMPING ATTACK MOVES PROVIDES AN ALMOST SINFUL ADVANTAGE OVER ENEMIES, WHICH SHOULD NOT BE IGNORED. THE FINAL BOSS BATTLE IS ALL ABOUT TARGETED JUMP MOVES, SO START PRACTICING!

CRUSH

ENRAGED

WHEN THE RAGE METER REACHES FULL CAPACITY YOU ENTER RAGE MODE. IN RAGE MODE EVERY ATTACK YOU MAKE DOLES OUT HIGHER LEVELS OF DAMAGE. SEE "RAGE MOVES" IN GAME BASICS FOR MORE INFORMATION.

After the battle, Bruce is awakened in his apartment by Professor Crawford's telephone call. Crawford calls to tell him he has finished the Gamma Orb and to come quickly before the military takes over the lab (the Orb is the key to cure Bruce Banner of the Gamma Ray disease). The sub-vocal earpiece that Bruce retrieves from the dumpster allows Crawford to vocally guide him in his trip to the lab.

ULTIMATE MEASURES

Professor Crawford's voice guides Banner to the laboratory via transmissions to a subvocal earpiece. Do not transform into the Hulk. Crawford cannot help you if you destroy the lab.

As Bruce enters the Gemini building's compound, his suspicion of Crawford's underlying purpose of help grows. He hasn't seen the guy in ten years! But Bruce's need overwhelms his previous, cautious feelings.

LOADING DOCK

You now control Bruce Banner, the calm human who must deal with the curse of the Hulk. His moves are more limited (see Bruce Banner Controls in Game Basics). Detection should be avoided and fighting isn't much of an option. You can defeat enemies with Bruce's limited fighting skills, but taking on more than one opponent is dangerous. Sneaking up behind a single opponent and putting him in a chokehold is the safest means to victory in hand-to-hand combat, but that's covered in a more appropriate level. This level should be cleared with stealth, not fisticuffs.

The Gemini building's loading dock is void of guards, head to the stairs and enter the building through the open door (**A**).

ANGRY

BRINGING OUT THE BEAST

WHEN BRUCE'S DAMAGE METER IS EMPTIED (AS A RESULT OF ENEMY ATTACKS), HE BECOMES ANGERED AND TURNS INTO THE HULK. IN THIS LEVEL, TURNING INTO THE HULK LEADS TO AN IMMEDIATE FAILURE FOR THE MISSION. ALL YOU SEE IS THE BEGINNINGS OF HIS TRANSFORMATION AND THE LEVEL ENDS.

GEMINI FLOOR 1

A short cutscene shows a guard behind a window and a few down the connecting hallway. Crouch and move forward to slip undetected past the window (**B**). Don't round the corner until you see the two guards from the connecting hallway enter the room behind the window.

Head up the stairs and a cinematic shows General Ryker and his forces have already arrived and are currently loading their trucks with lab property. After the cinematic, walk up to the elevator switch (**C**) and open the elevator doors. If you were followed to the top of the stairs, this cinematic will not begin and you will not be able to enter the elevator afterwards.

General Ryker

Press ◉

HACKING THE DOOR LOCK CODE

Crawford temporarily disables the security camera on the following floor (**D**). Crouch and walk (or run and roll) under the security window (**E**). At the end of the connecting hallway is computer (**F**) that holds the password that unlocks the adjacent door. These computer code-busting puzzles occur throughout the game and progressively get tougher by limiting the time to hack the password.

Walk up to the computer and access the code screen. There are two rows of numbers and letters (called "digits" from here on). The top row is a random display that must be matched via manipulating the lower row. You have 20 seconds to complete this challenge. If you fail, log onto the computer and try again.

Press left and right to move the cursor. Pressing the button that appears under the selected digits swaps the positions of the digits that appear in the 2-digit selection cursor. Look at the first digit in the top row and find it on the bottom row. Move the selector so that the digit you want appears on the *right* side of the 2-digit selector. Pressing the correct button moves the digit one slot to the *left*. Continue to move the cursor to the left, highlighting the desired digit with the *right* side of the selector slot until it lines up with the matching digit on the top row. Repeat this process with each digit to complete the code. This is the process used to break all the computer codes faced in the game. The quicker you can perform these moves the better prepared you will be for future puzzles.

In the next room is a stack of crates on the left side of the entrance. Walk into the green arrows behind the crates (**G**) and remain there until the two guards in the room exit through the door you just entered. They return in time, so move to the left end of the room quickly. Find the stack of crates along the left wall that can be moved (a green targeting arrow appears on the crates as you near them). Pull the crates away from the open vent, then let go of the crates and head around them to the open vent (**H**). A cutscene takes you through the vent and into the office (**I**) on the other side of the wall.

SMASH

TIME FOR PRACTICE

IF YOU'RE FEELING CONFIDENT, EXPERIMENT WITH THE CHOKE-HOLD IN THIS ROOM. IT'S THE FIRST AREA WHERE YOU CAN SAFELY USE IT. RUNNING TO THE SHELVES AT THE REAR OF THE LAB ALLOWS YOU TO SNEAK UP ON ONE OF THE PATROLLING GUARDS AND SILENTLY TAKE HIM OUT. TAKE OUT THE SECOND GUARD AS HE MOVES TO LEAVE THE ROOM.

ELEVATOR SWITCH ROOM

Walk up to the window that overlooks the multi-storied room below. The Gamma Orb Laboratory below can be seen as Bruce continues to struggle with his apprehensive thoughts of Crawford and his sudden urge to assist with his disease. Walk up to the elevator (**J**) and pull the switches on either side. Walk up to the elevator's button and use it to gain access the lower floor.

HACKING INTO THE GAMMA ORB CHAMBER

Head to the computer (**K**) in the back corner of the room that overlooks the Gamma Orb Lab and begin the GRS lock challenge. Use the same tactics as you did earlier to hack this 8-digit code that will unlock the lab's sterile airlock door. You have 20 seconds to complete the challenge.

Once the door is unlocked, enter the now-opened sterile airlock (**L**). A cinematic takes you into the Gamma Orb Lab where the Professor uses his machine to suck the Gamma Radiation from Bruce and capture it inside an orb. Bruce discovers that his suspicions were justified as the professor uses Bruce's Gamma to infect his own crippled body, creating a stronger, bigger, and corrupt monster. The altered beast inside the professor is Ravage!

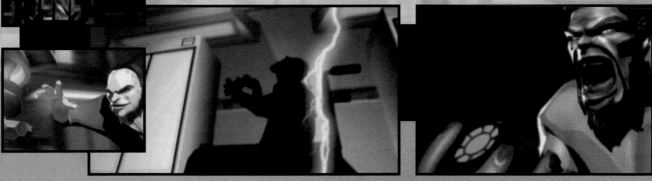

27

Professor Crawford has betrayed Banner and misused the power of the Hulk to mutate himself. With a fraction of the Hulk's power captured in his Gamma Orb, he flees the scene in his new mutated form, known as "Ravage."

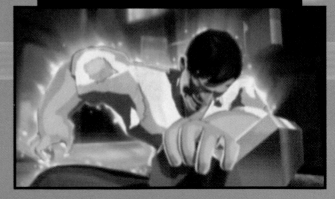

ROOFTOP CLAMBER

This level involves following the trail of Ravage's destruction across many San Francisco rooftops. Along the way, many of Ryker's soldiers confront the Hulk. Fighting these troops is completely optional as escaping from the rooftop is just a matter of finding the exit used by Ravage. There's no time limit, so have fun and smash some soldiers with the many interactive objects found on the rooftops. The flow of soldiers seems almost endless, so at some point, break away from the fights and continue to follow Ravage's trail. There are quite a few areas where a certain number of soldiers must be defeated in order to make the green directional arrows appear that help you find the exit. This does not mean you can't exit the area before the arrows appear! Just find the area of each rooftop or room that looks like the area that Ravage left through and jump in pursuit.

CRUSH

CLEARING A PATH

THE FASTEST WAY TO MOVE THROUGH THE WORLD IS TO DASH AND DASH PUNCH. THIS QUICKLY CLEARS ANY FLIMSY WALLS OR GLASS OUT OF THE HULK'S PATH. YOU CAN ALSO TOSS OBJECTS OR ENEMIES AT THE GLASS TO DAMAGE IT.

AREA 1: ROOFTOP (A)

The first rooftop has two air-condition units and a vent shaft that can be picked up and used as weapons against the soldiers that pour out of the single doorway. Walk up to the arrows near the work-free health power-up and jump (or walk) over the edge to access the next building.

AREA 2: ROOFTOP (B)

The second rooftop has three sections, the first part you land on, a glass-enclosed sunroom, and beyond that is another area that is exactly like the first (objects and everything). The first section where you land has a large condenser unit that can be used as a weapon and a rusty pipe in the corner. The Shock Troopers pour out of the doorway. Knocking the soldiers over the edge of the building is fun, but you miss out on the fruits of your labor. The power-ups left behind are beyond reach.

Smash through the glass to enter the sunroom (**C**) or enter the opening on the right. The sunroom has three tables that can be used to smash the soldiers that issue from the second doorway.

The area beyond the sunroom (**D**) is almost exactly like the first area on this floor except for the vent in the corner that can be used as a weapon. Ravage's point of departure is marked with glowing green arrows through the broken half wall. Jump while near the green arrows to leave this rooftop. It's a heck of a long jump that requires a cool cinematic.

4 HITS FIERCE!!

Press Ⓐ to jump to the next rooftop.

AREA 3: BUILDING INTERIOR (E)

The jump from the rooftops leads through the window of an office building. Inside are tables that can be picked up and used to beat the soldiers that spill out of the elevators in either short hallway. The large crumbled wall pieces can also be picked up and used as weapons.

Head to the room beyond the elevators, face the broken window, then jump to the next rooftop.

SMASH

BASHING WALLS

THIS IS NOT A TRICK, BUT YOU JUST HAVE TO PUNCH WALLS IN SOME OF THESE AREAS. IT'S VERY COOL THAT YOU CAN CRACK ANY SURFACE THAT YOU PUNCH! TRY IT ON THE WALL TO THE RIGHT AS YOU ENTER THIS BUILDING TO OPEN UP THE SECOND HALLWAY AND ELEVATOR ACCESS.

AREA 4: ROOFTOP WITH HELICOPTER (F)

As you enter the rooftop where a helicopter hovers overhead, grab one of the rusty poles or the condenser unit and jump and throw the object with the helicopter targeted to bring it down. Soldiers are present, and more descend from the helicopter if you don't bring it down. Of course this is all optional, as you can escape the attack by breaking through the glass wall at the other end of the rooftop.

AREA 5: LOWER ROOFTOP (G)

The lower rooftop beyond the glass wall contains a couple condenser units, a ventilation shaft and a rusty pipe that can be used to pummel the air-dropped Shock Troopers.
Head to the far end of the rooftop and find a Health power-up near a cracked window. Break through the window to access the following rooftop.

AREA 6: EVEN LOWER ROOFTOP (H)

This narrow rooftop contains two vent shafts, two condensers and two rusty pipes. The area remains infested with soldiers that descend from the helicopters. The Helicopter flies much lower and is much easier to see in this level and the last rooftop level, making it much easier to target with one of the heavy rooftop-objects. After a satisfactory amount of destruction, jump down into the following building.

AREA 7: BUILDING INTERIOR (I)

The building with the wood paneled interior houses four large wooden crates, two pipes, and a table. The cement columns crumble under heavy hands, and can be used as weapons (looks cool when you tear them up, too). This is one of those areas mentioned earlier that the green directional arrows wont appear in until you defeat a certain number of soldiers. The soldiers enter the room through one of two elevators. Defeat eight soldiers and the green arrows appear in front of the cracked window on the far side of the room.

SMASH

EARLY ESCAPE

THE GLASS WHERE THE EXIT ARROWS APPEAR CANNOT BE BROKEN. IF YOU'VE PLAYED THIS LEVEL BEFORE AND KNOW WHERE THE ARROWS APPEAR, THEN YOU CAN EASILY EXIT THE ROOM BEFORE THE DEFEATING ANY SOLDIERS AND BEFORE THE GREEN ARROWS APPEAR. IF JUMP BEFORE YOU REACH THE CRACKED GLASS (A FEW STEPS BACK FROM THE GLASS) YOU CAN EXIT THE ROOM EARLY!

AREA 8: ROOFTOP (J)

This area immediately fills with Rifle Soldiers pouring out of the elevator. Pick up one of the three tables in the room to pound them between the floor tiles. Smash through the glass wall to find a condenser unit on one end of the rooftop and a vent shaft on the other. Battle through the Rifle Soldiers and pick up the Health power-up along the back wall. Enter the green arrow to access the next rooftop.

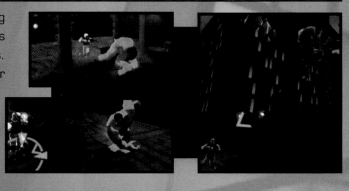

SMASH

SMASH

USING SMASH WHEN HOLDING A LARGE OBJECT (SUCH AS THE CONDENSER UNITS, VENT SHAFTS, AND CARS) DEFEATS THE SOLDIERS WITH ON HIT. THE OBJECT SHOULD WITHSTAND QUITE A FEW ATTACK USES BEFORE IT DISINTEGRATES, WHICH MAKES THROWING IT AT ONE ENEMY SOMEWHAT WASTEFUL.

AREA 9: ROOFTOP (K)

This balcony looks just like the one you just left. There are more Rifle Soldiers to greet the Hulk's arrival. These guys are still rappelling out of the helicopter heard overhead. Use the condenser unit, or one of the rusty pipes to fend them off. Run through the elevator room to reach the balcony on the other end of the building that has similar pummeling objects and the green arrow (L) to the next building.

AREA 10: PARKING GARAGE (M)

Inside the garage are more cool crumbling columns (once completely broken, the sections can be picked up), two wall condenser units, two cars and tons of Shock Troopers. The exit is on the far left side of the room and is available whenever the Hulk enters the broken wall section.

Jump from rooftop to pursue Ravage.

AREA 11: PARKING GARAGE II (N)

Leaving the first parking lot leads to another almost identical garage. However, in this garage there's only one car, but much more rubble to pick up. Stick around to defeat some Rifle Soldiers or smash the doorway on the left wall and jump down to the alley below to complete the level.

Crawford/Ravage has fled into the city sewer system. The military is now on full alert and intent on stopping both of him and the Hulk. Pursue Ravage and destroy his Gamma Orb.

SEWER CATACOMBS

This level involves following Ravage through the sewer and catacombs beneath the city while fighting different class soldiers in Ryker's military. You won't catch up to Ravage in this level, but you do encounter a new mutation. The altered and ugly Gamma Dogs make their grand appearance in this dark, damp underworld.

SMASH

ESCAPING BATTLES

UNTIL REACHING A COUPLE UNIQUE CHAMBERS NEAR THE END OF THE LEVEL, THERE IS NOTHING STOPPING YOU FROM RUNNING FROM FIGHTS AND THROUGH ALL THE PASSAGEWAYS AND CATACOMBS. IT'S NOT AS FUN, BUT IT IS AN OPTION. THE BREAKABLE FLOODGATES THAT SEPARATE SECTIONS OF THE SEWER CAN BE BROKEN THE MOMENT THEY'RE APPROACHED. IF YOU WANT TO GET THROUGH THE LEVEL IN A HURRY, RUN PAST THE ENEMY, DEFEATING ONLY THE ONES THAT GET IN YOUR PATH. THE HEALTH POWER-UPS THEY DROP HELP YOU THROUGH AS MANY ENEMIES GIVE CHASE AND CONTINUE TO FIRE THEIR WEAPONS.

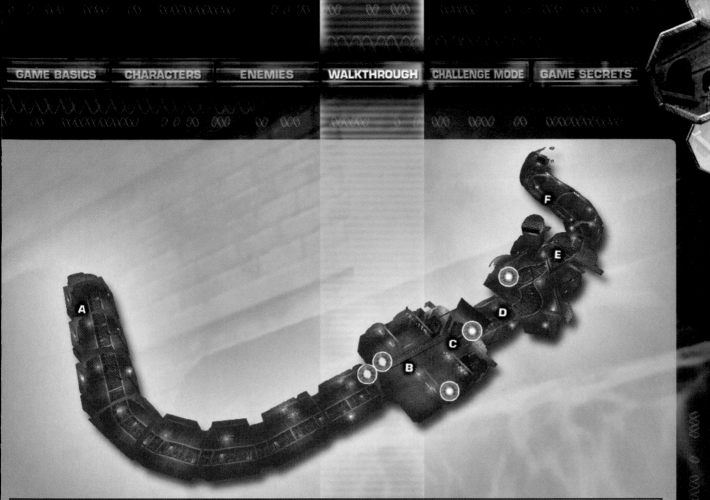

SEWER PASSAGEWAY (A)

Ravage can be seen and heard laughing at the far end of the first sewage passageway. His health meter appears at the top of the screen, but there's no need to deplete it, you cannot defeat Ravage in this level. Besides, the low overhangs jutting from the ceiling prevent you from throwing many objects far enough to hit him. Your goal now is to chase him, not defeat him. At the end of the first passageway is a large metal floodgate that must be destroyed to gain access to the first catacomb.

CATACOMB 07-A: GAMMA DOG BATTLE

Upon entering the first catacomb (**B**), a cinematic shows three Gamma Dogs creeping up from behind while Ravage escapes the chamber. Pick up the Rage power-up near the barrel, then use the explosive barrels in the chamber to Smash the Gamma Dogs. The last hit of a barrel results in a huge explosion that can damage multiple enemies.

CRUSH

GRAPPLE WITH GAMMA DOGS

GAMMA DOGS CANNOT BE LIFTED, MAKING GRAPPLE MOVES IMPOSSIBLE. WHEN YOU TRY TO PICK UP A TRANSMUTED MUTT, A UNIQUE MOVE IS EXECUTED. THE HULK GRABS THE DOG BY THE NECK AND PUNTS IT IN THE HEAD!

Use large combos, such as Overhead Smash, Dashing Punch, or Right Jab to take on the Gamma Dogs. After defeating the three Gamma Dogs a continual barrage of four soldiers (2 Shock and 2 Rifle) swing into the chamber from the catwalk above (if you don't take out the Gamma Dogs quickly enough, the soldiers appear while you're fighting them). While using jumping moves, don't waste time charging the attacks in midair or the Dogs may jump up and bite. This not only causes harm but also interrupts the attack. Use the pipes, crates, and barrels to pummel the bald canines. When you've had enough of the battle with the soldiers, smash through the floodgate (**C**), grab the major Health power-up and head through the passageway to the next chamber.

CATACOMB 77-C: GAMMA DOG AMBUSH (D)

Enter the second chamber, immediately pick up the explosive barrels and throw them at the soldiers rappelling from the catwalk in the distance. Keep moving to avoid a dual Gamma Dog attack. They sneak up from behind through the previous passageway and are actually faster than the Hulk. Throw barrels into the crowd of Rifle Soldiers and Gamma Dogs. Bust through the next floodgate (**E**) when the forces have been softened.

PASSAGEWAY BETWEEN 77-D AND 31-D

In the passageway between catacomb (77-C) and the next (31-D) Ravage can be seen charging through Ryker's soldiers, continuing his escape through the sewer. The first encounter with Shockshielders occurs in this passageway (**F**). These soldiers hold electrified stun batons and portable shield generators. Touching their plasma shields presents the same danger as being hit by their stun batons. The Hulk cannot punch through the plasma shields and Sonic Clap does little help to shut them down. Find objects to hit or throw at the plasma shields to temporarily shut them down, or wait for a soldier to shut it down (which usually means he is preparing a stun attack). When the plasma shield is down, quickly move in and bash the soldier before he has a chance to raise the plasma shield. Using explosive barrels on groups of Shockshielders works splendidly.

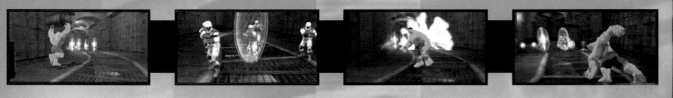

CATACOMB (G)

Missile Soldiers are deployed on the catwalk on the opposite side of the chamber in catacomb (**G**). Missile Soldiers are just as bad, if not worse than the Shockshielders. Being hit by a missile is no picnic. It causes major damage and prevents charged jump moves. The missiles are not guided (just well-aimed) so if you move from your current location when you hear a missile being fired, it is easily avoided. The difficulty with these soldiers occurs when they attack in numbers or in conjunction with other enemies. When Missile Soldiers are present in a room, they should become priority number one. Throw barrels, or crates at the soldiers and bust through the following floodgate (**H**) before you are snowed under with Shockshielders, Rifle, and more Missile Soldiers.

MISSILE CANAL

Between Catacomb (**G**) and the large canal chamber (**J**) is a small passageway with three Shockshielders (**I**). Use the crates and other objects in the room to douse the plasma shields and flatten the soldiers.

Break through the following floodgate and enter the canal area (**I**). On the opposite side of the canal (**K**) are four Missile Soldiers who begin firing the moment the Hulk enters the chamber. Pick up the crates or barrels and target the Missile Soldiers or the nearby explosive barrels.

Keep moving as much as possible between picking up barrels and targeting the enemy to avoid the incoming projectiles. The missiles shot from the rocket launchers can be punched back to the soldiers, but using the projectiles at hand to destroy the enemy is safer and quicker.

Guarding the exit on your side of the canal are two Shockshielders (**L**). Pick up more crates or barrels and let 'em have it. Smash through the floodgate they guard and continue past a few more to pass through a few small passageways (**M**). Beyond the third floodgate the enemy appears again. A Gamma Dog and four Shock Soldiers attack, with more following when the first gang is defeated (**N**). Upon entering the room, pick up the large club to the right. On the left side of the room (**O**) is a large hole in the floor. Jump into the hole to continue the pursuit of Ravage.

LOWER CATACOMB (P)

Drop from the hole in the floor above into the catacombs. A text message warns that to progress, you must defeat the enemy. There is no way to escape the room until you defeat twelve Rifle Soldiers. Use the crates and area attacks to quickly snuff the threat.

With that done, a large explosion rips a hole in the back wall. Before heading through the hole, pick up another explosive barrel and fling it at the approaching Shockshielders. Beyond the Shockshielders is a gang of Missile Soldiers (Q). Jump over their missiles (and their heads) and continue, or squash the soldiers with mighty green fists. Smash through the final floodgate to begin the final sewer battle.

FINAL SEWER BATTLE

The final chamber (R) is littered with pipes, crates, explosive barrels, and Rifle and Missile Soldiers. This is a fun battle, and not too difficult with the amount of objects available for battle. The key is to take out the Missile Soldiers before dealing with the less damaging Rifle Soldiers. Keep moving to avoid the missiles as they are being shot from all directions. Use the explosive barrels as much as possible. The concussions from their detonations take out multiple enemies. After a few waves of troops have been defeated, approach the dark doorway towards the back of the room to exit the sewer and conclude the level.

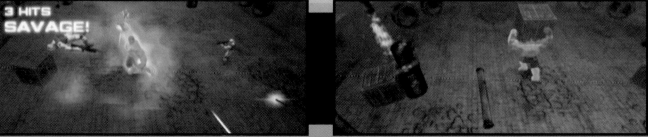

Ravage has escaped the sewer system, leaving you to deal with the remaining military forces. Fight or flee, but find a way to pick up Ravage's trail.

TRAIN STATION

This level could be completed in under a minute if you rip through the train stations and jump to the exit without fighting any enemies, but what kind of fun would that be? The train depot is one long, continual area separated by metal hangar doors and a lower depot section accessed via a short shaft. The following is a breakdown of the areas: enemies faced, plus objects on hand that can be used to inflict pain.

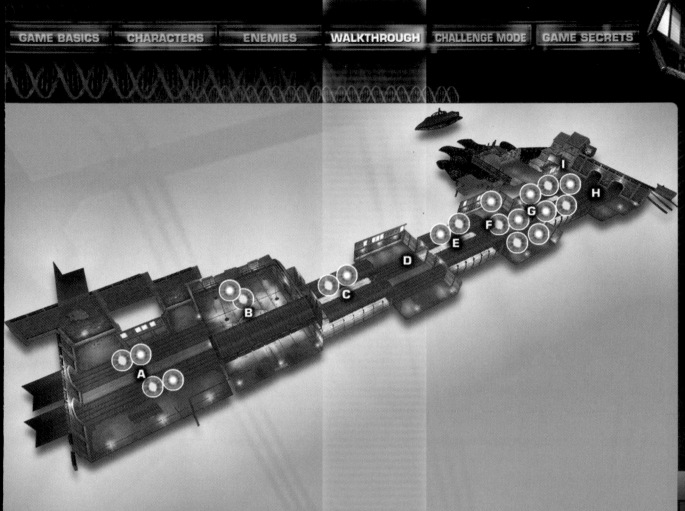

DEPOT I

About 30 seconds into the level, a Gamma Dog bites through the hangar door and attacks teeth first. Rifle Soldiers and Shockshielders soon flood the area (**A**). The area is filled with items to smash and to use as weapons. The trains poking out of tunnels can be blown up but not picked up. The train cars that sit in the middle of the area can be picked up and used as an awesome crushing tool, but must first be broken apart with a few punches. What remains is a large broken section that is excellent for squashing multiple enemies at once. After destroying a train car, a Rage and a Health power-up appear in its place. This occurs throughout the level.

There are crates and water pipes along the walls, a dumpster in a nook, and a heavy forklift. Use all of them to obliterate the opposing forces. Once the area has been cleared, punch through the thin metal doors and enter the depot. Inside is much of the same as outside: Gamma Dogs, Rifle Soldiers, and Shockshielders. Pick up and use the crates, train cars, forklifts, barrels, pipes and ductwork. When the enemy has been punished enough, punch through the metal doors and drop down to the lower train station area.

DEPOT 2

The lower Depot (**C**) contains a train car, large wooden strut beams, crates, and barrels to use against the Shock Soldiers and Shockshielders that attack inside this structure. Break the support beams and take the large shard for the most durable weapon in the building. After mopping up, break through the sheet metal doors and head outside.

Outside the second Depot (**D**) is a large tower that can be broken down and the very large pieces that remain can be picked up! Now that's a big human swatter! There are also explosive barrels, a forklift in a corner, crates scattered about, and a pipe.

DEPOT 3

Head through the third Depot (**E**) (which has more train cars, wooden support beams, ductwork, barrels, and crates) while fending off the Gamma Dogs and soldiers to the next outdoor area (**F**). This area is a carbon copy of the previous area, big towers and all.

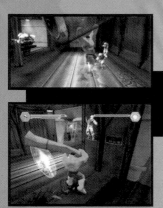

DEPOT 4

The fourth Depot (**G**) is crowded with more train cars than the previous shelters, and the barrels, crates, and wooden beams continue to appear. Break through the metal doors on the opposite end to reach the *End Of The Line* (**H**). The welcoming committee includes Gamma Dogs and Shockshielders. Use the large towers, forklifts, and barrels to crush the enemy, then head to the far left corner (**I**) to jump over the short fence to the area below.

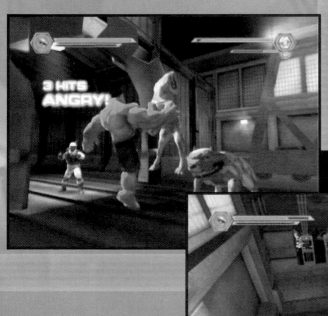

A DIFFERENT BREED

After the Hulk escapes the military, the energy vampire known as Half-Life has set up an ambush. Avoid direct contact with him as his touch transfers health from the Hulk to Half-Life.

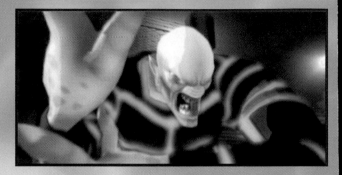

HALF-LIFE

HALF-LIFE, A MUTANT PARASITIC VAMPIRE, AMBUSHES HULK AT THE END OF THE TRAIN LINE. HALF-LIFE SPILLS THE BEANS AND REVEALS THAT RAVAGE HAS TAKEN THE ORB TO ALCATRAZ. IN CLASSIC VILLAIN STYLE, HE SHARES THIS INFORMATION WITH THE ASSUMPTION THAT IT WON'T LEAVE THIS SITE. HE OBVIOUSLY HASN'T READ ENOUGH COMIC BOOKS.

BOSS ATTRIBUTES

HALF-LIFE IS A SLIPPERY, BOUNCY, AND QUITE SHOCKING FELLOW WITH THE ABILITY TO DRAIN LIFE ENERGY ON CONTACT. HE'S EXTREMELY FAST AND THE HULK IS NOT ABLE TO KEEP PACE. HALF-LIFE HAS A JUMPING KICK ATTACK, A 2-HANDED SHOCK ATTACK, A NUMBER OF LIFE-SUCKING GRAB ATTACKS, AND A MOVE WHERE HE HOLDS THE HULK'S ARM WITH HIS LEFT HAND, SMACKS WITH THE RIGHT, THEN FINISHES WITH A BACKHAND! HALF-LIFE HAS TWO HEALTH METERS (DRAIN HIS HEALTH METER ONCE AND IT FILLS ONE MORE TIME). IT'S NOT POSSIBLE TOUCH HALF-LIFE WITHOUT TAKING DAMAGE. YOU MUST FIND A WAY TO DEFEAT HIM WITHOUT TOUCHING HIM.

THE BATTLE ENVIRONMENT

USE THE OBJECTS AROUND THE ARENA TO THROW, POUND, AND ELECTRIFY HALF-LIFE. THERE ARE WOODEN CRATES, METAL SHIPPING CONTAINERS, LARGE PIPES, FUEL TANKS, AND A FORK-LIFT. IN ADDITION, HEALTH POWER-UPS CAN BE FOUND IN SOME OF THE WOODEN CRATES. HEALTH POWER-UPS AND THE INTER-ACTIVE OBJECTS USED AS WEAPONS REGENERATE IN TIME.

ALL FOUR SIDES OF THE ARENA HAVE A FENCED-IN GENERA-TOR. BREAK THE FENCE FROM AROUND THE GENERATOR AND THE GENERATOR BECOMES ELECTRICALLY CHARGED. IF TOUCHED, THIS CHARGE DOES A SMALL AMOUNT OF DAMAGE. ELECTRIFYING THE VAMPIRE (KNOCK HIM INTO CONTACT WITH THESE GENERATORS) FRIES HIM, DRAINING UP TO A QUARTER OF HIS HEALTH!

THE BATTLE

KNOCKING HALF-LIFE INTO THE GENERATORS IS THE KEY TO A QUICK DEFEAT. IT'S POSSIBLE TO WEAR HIM DOWN WITH THROWN OBJECTS AND CRUSHING FORKLIFT ATTACKS, BUT KNOCKING HIM INTO THE CHARGED GENERATORS MAKES SHORT WORK OF THIS BOSS. FIRST, KNOCK AWAY THE FENCES FROM AROUND THE GENERATORS TO OPEN ACCESS TO THEM.

FIND A WEAPON, SUCH AS A LONG PIPE, AND LURE HALF-LIFE IN FRONT OF A GENERATOR. USE THE TARGET BUTTON TO SELECT HALF-LIFE AS THE TARGET OF WEAPONS. KNOCK HIM TOWARDS THE GENERATOR WITH THE HELD OBJECT. IT'S POSSIBLE TO JUGGLE THE BOSS ONCE HE'S AIRBORNE. HIT HIM ONCE, THEN STEP FORWARD AND HIT HIM AGAIN IN MIDAIR. FOUR OF THESE GENERATOR-ASSISTED ATTACKS COMPLETELY DRAIN HIS LIFE METER.

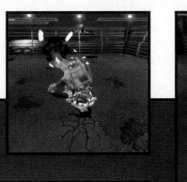

SMASH

SUPER SONIC CLAP

IF THE HULK HAPPENS TO ENTER RAGE MODE, USE SUPER SONIC CLAP TO KNOCK HALF-LIFE INTO THE GENERATORS. THIS ATTACK IS POWERFUL AND THROWS THE BOSS GREAT DISTANCES.

ONCE HALF-LIFE'S HEALTH HAS BEEN DEPLETED, HE PULLS HIMSELF TOGETHER, FILLS HIS LIFE METER TO THE MAX, AND BEGINS THE SECOND PHASE OF THE BATTLE. THIS TIME, HALF-LIFE GLOWS WITH ELECTRICITY. HIS ATTACKS REMAIN THE SAME, AND SO SHOULD THE STRATEGY TO DEFEAT HIM. KEEP KNOCKING HIM TOWARDS THE GENERATORS AND IT SOON ENDS FOR THE ELECTRIC VAMPIRE.

HALF-LIFE

INFILTRATION

The Hulk is physically exhausted from the shocking fight with Half-Life and has lapsed back into Bruce Banner. Half-Life told him that Ravage and the Orb have escaped to Alcatraz. Bruce must stealthily penetrate the fortress and do his best to remain human. The facility is rigged with multiple Gamma detection units. If the Hulk is detected the hostage, Betty Ross, will be terminated.

Infiltrate the facility.
The enemy has a hostage. You cannot afford to be seen.

ALCATRAZ

BREAKING INTO ALCATRAZ

The Leader's paramilitary units, the Alpha Guard and Gamma Dogs, enforce the security at this facility. Adding to these obstacles are the many spotlights around the compound. Step into the light and it's all over! Alpha Guards continually advance and Bruce is no fighter.

From the beginning (**A**), dash to the left to hide behind the first truck (**B**) and allow the three Alpha Guards to pass the trucks. As soon as the third guard passes the front of the truck, run around the front of the second truck. While avoiding the spotlight, work toward the Gamma Dog pen behind the spotlight towers (**C**).

SNEAKING PAST SLEEPING GAMMA DOGS

The second spotlight moves in and out of the Gamma Dog pen. As soon as it moves out of the pen, push the single crate to the stack of crates in the corner. Release the crate and clamber up to the crates and onto the storage container in the dog pen (**D**).

Walk off the edge of the container and press the Crouch button when Banner's feet hit the ground. Hold the Crouch button down while walking through the Gamma Dog pen to silently sneak past the sleeping beasts. Sneak all the way around the pen to the stack of crates (**E**) next to the second storage container—pausing to allow the light to pass if necessary. Clamber up the crates and a cutscene shows the distant generator switch that must be reached.

BLACKOUT

In this fenced in area are two Alpha Guards and more Gamma Dogs sleeping in cages. Jump down and run to the generator switch [F] before the guard's patrol takes him to this end of the compound. Avoid the spotlight, walk up to the generator switch and turn off the spotlights.

The blackout alerts the two guards and they quickly investigate. Run behind the nearby crates and crouch down as the closest guard faces the generator (behind the crates are two large Health power-ups). Sneak out from behind the crates, creep up behind him before he moves, and press the Action button to get the guard in a chokehold. The further away the guard was when the switch was pulled, the more time it takes him to approach this area. If you continue being spotted before having the chance to hide, quickly run to the switch from the dog pen using a more direct route.

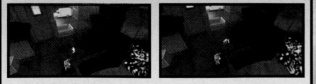

SMASH

I'M A SCIENTIST NOT A FIGHTER!

ELIMINATING AN ALPHA GUARD IN HAND-TO-HAND COMBAT IS NOT IMPOSSIBLE, BUT THE TASK IS TOUGHER WITH MULTIPLE GUARDS. THE KEY IS TO QUICKLY KNOCK DOWN ANY GUARD WITH BASIC PUNCHES, RUNNING AROUND HIM SO THAT WHEN HE GETS UP YOU ARE BEHIND HIM, THEN SUCKER PUNCH HIM AGAIN. CONTINUE UNTIL HE DOESN'T GET UP AGAIN. WHEN THE ALPHA GUARD IS GIVEN A CHANCE TO SHOOT WITH HIS OICW RIFLE (OR USE IT AS A CLUB IN CLOSE) IT'S HARD TO GET BACK INTO A GOOD FIGHTING DISTANCE.

CAUSING A GUARD TO WHIFF WITH A SWUNG RIFLE OR A RISING KICK ATTACK IS A GOOD WAY TO BAIT-AND-HIT THESE GUYS. IT'S ALSO WORTH TRYING BANNER'S SURRENDER TECHNIQUE. WHEN A GUARD CALLS OUT FOR BANNER TO FREEZE, TRY FREEZING! THE SOLDIER WON'T SHOOT, BUT INSTEAD APPROACHES AND QUESTIONS BANNER. THIS REMOVES THE ENEMY'S ADVANTAGE OF RANGE, MEANING BANNER CAN CONFRONT THE ENEMY IN HAND-TO-HAND COMBAT OR FLOOR HIM, THEN RUN AND HIDE.

SMASH

ESCAPING AFTER BEING SPOTTED

WHENEVER YOU HAVE BEEN SPOTTED, RUN A CERTAIN DISTANCE OR DUCK AROUND A CORNER TO LOSE THE ATTACKER, THEN REENTER STEALTH MODE. WHEN YOU REACH AN APPROPRIATE DISTANCE, A CHORD CHIMES AND SOMETIMES BRUCE SAYS THAT HE'S LOST THEM.

The second guard patrols the area (**G**) between the spotlight tower and the truck passed on the way to the generator switch. Look through the mesh of the tower to see it, and the guard won't spot you in that hiding spot. Get behind the guard and give him the chokehold. If the lights are back on, hit the generator switch again and wait for the other guard to return. Use the crates next to the tower to hide before the ambush.

There is a Continue power-up behind these crates. Once both Alpha Guards have been dealt with, run past the Gamma Dog cages and head to the right at the T intersection.

LEFT OR RIGHT AT THE "T"

Jump over the large fence via the left or right route—each route contains a spotlight tower and crates that allow passage over the fence. The right route (right from the camera angle before reaching the intersection; left from the turned overhead camera angle when in the intersection) leads to another Continue and a Health power-up. The left route holds a Health power-up.

Wait for the spotlight to move and push the single crate up against the stack and use the stack as stairs to hop over the fence (**H**). To the left is the Continue and Health power-up behind a couple of crates. Head around the building and put the Guard (**I**) in a chokehold.

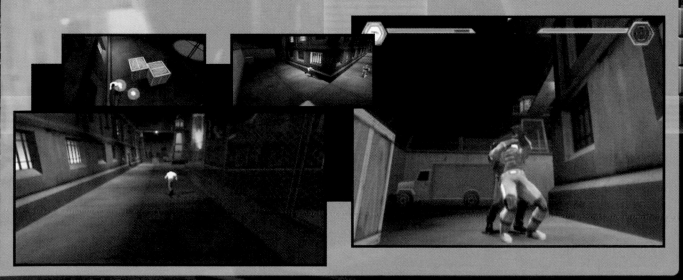

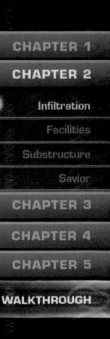

FINDING THE SECOND GENERATOR SWITCH

Run to the large open compound, hugging the right wall. Head around the left corner, hide behind the crates (**J**) and make a break straight back for the large building (**K**). Instead of heading right into the generator yard (**O**), head left and stay close to the building front to avoid detection by the two guards in the distance.

Head around the corner and continue to hug the building while creeping around the back of the parked truck (**L**). Allow the nearby guard to leave the area and head to the left corner of the fences when the spotlight clears. Remain in the corner (**M**) until the spotlight passes (it will not shine in the fence corner), then head back to the generator switch area (**N**).

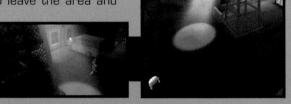

When the spotlight is gone, pull the large stack of crates back to the green arrows in the back of the area up against the fence. Return to the single crate and pull it to the stack of crates just moved and make steps to hop over into the generator yard. Inside the generator yard is Health power-up. Activate the generator switch to open the gate to your yard and the gate to the last generator switch (**O**).

GENERATOR SWITCH 3

If you move as soon as you throw the switch, following the same route in front of the large building on the way to the next generator yard, you can make it without detection. If you hesitate, a guard investigates the area and you may have to eliminate him before continuing.

Avoid the spotlight near the last generator switch (**O**) in the same fashion as before—using the corner fences as a safe area from the light. Dash into the open yard and take the Continue power-up and any of the five major Health power-ups as necessary.

ENTERING THE BUILDING

The switch opens the massive door to the building between the generators. Enter this door and at the end of the hallway is another Universal Code Input terminal.

In the following room, two Alpha Guards patrol the second floor hallways that overlook the large room. Stick to the left wall and follow it around, then quickly enter the computer room before the guard on the upper-right walkway begins his patrol. Use Free Look to spot this guard. If he is watching, wait for him to leave before attempting to run forward and round the wall to enter the computer room.

BREAKING THE FFS GAMMA DETECTION CODE

Walk up to the terminal in the back of the small room and begin the digit matching challenge. Completing the challenge successfully shuts down the Gamma detectors, allowing Banner to continue through Alcatraz as the Hulk without being detected. Use the same strategy used to beat the door lock challenges in "Desperate Measures" earlier. It's the same concept. There are 20 seconds to match 10 random digits. The code is longer but the time remains the same.

Once the code is hacked, a cinematic shows Madman threatening Betty in another room. This enrages Bruce and brings out the beast in him.

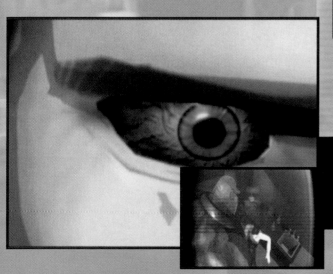

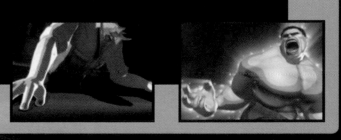

With the Gamma Detection System shut down, the Hulk can do battle without endangering Betty Ross. Level the defenses and smash through to her rescue.

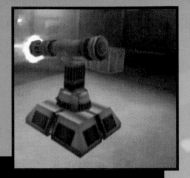

ROOM (A)

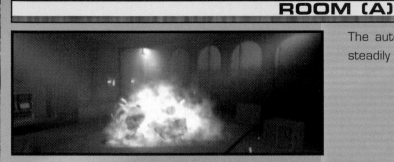

The autogun seen at the end of the last level begins steadily firing at the Hulk.

Punch the autogun six or seven times to destroy it, but a few charged punches (or single strike with an object) should finish the job faster. Its insignificant rounds don't inflict much damage. Inside the room are many large wooden crates and a steady flow of Alpha Guards. Grab the crates and use them on the guards. The autogun, after being destroyed, splits into two pummeling weapons. These metal objects are more durable than the wooden crates. Use area attacks such as Gamma Crusher, Gamma Stomp, and Sonic Clap.

If you need more Health and Rage power-ups than the Alpha Guards provide, smash the regenerating crates. A Super Sonic Clap destroys everything in the room and reveals all the power-ups. The power-ups continue to regenerate as well, so there's no reason to leave slightly wounded.

HALLWAY (B)

Break through the small door in the hallway and take a right at the T intersection (follow the sign on the wall that points to C-12). The hallway to the left is protected by a force field. Break through two more small doors and battle the Alpha Guards. Break through the last door in the right hallway to enter the generator room. Multiple Sonic Claps work well on the Alpha Guards in this narrow passageway.

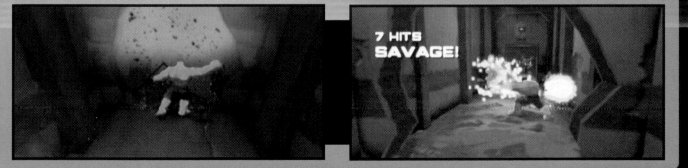

7 HITS
SAVAGE!

GENERATOR ROOM (C)

Gamma Dogs and more Alpha Guards patrol the Generator Room. Backing up into the previous hallway allows the enemy to come closer, thus enabling the Hulk to avoid a fight inside the small room. Inside the room, use the large chunks of wall, and a few crates, to flatten the enemy. Destroying the generator shuts down the force field in the hallway. Before leaving the generator room, break all the crates for Rage and Health power-ups.

HALLWAY (B)

Now that the generator is gone and the force field blocking the left passageway at the T intersection is down, head through hallway C-10. Battle the Alpha Guards, break down the dividing walls, and head into the room at the end. Use Sonic Claps (or a Super Sonic Clap when enraged) and chunks of wall to clear the hallway of enemies.

ROOM (D)

The room at the end of the left hallway contains Alpha Shielders. These are similar to Ryker's Shockshielders, only tougher to defeat once their shields are down. Use the large wall chunk to smash the closest Alpha Shielders. One hit won't eliminate them and they will get back on their feet. There is very little to pick up in the room, so another tactic is needed to defeat them. If you get close to the Shielders, they eventually lower their shields to attack. Rush in and squash them when that happens. The computer terminals along the walls can be destroyed for Health power-ups (they appear a few seconds after destroying them, so be patient). Break through the glass wall in the back of the room to drop down into Room E.

CAFETERIA (E)

Inside the large cafeteria are many picnic tables, large chunks of wall, and cement columns that can be used to bruise the Gamma Dogs, Alpha Guards, and Alpha Missiles. Try to take out the Gamma Dogs first (while continually moving to avoid the rockets), then concentrate on the Alpha Missiles.
Head through the doorway to enter Cafeteria F.

CAFETERIA (F)

There's not much in the second cafeteria except more picnic tables and any enemies that followed from the previous room. The trouble area is the connecting hallway from this room into the walk-in cooler. Gamma Dog after Gamma Dog pours into the hallway as you attempt to enter the cooler. Draw back into the cafeteria and use the picnic tables to ground the doggies and, with fists flying, push through into the cooler.

MEAT COOLER (G)

Knock down the meat from the meat hooks and use them to finish off the Gamma Dogs and Alpha Soldiers. Break down the door and head into the following hallway.

HALLWAY (H)

Exit the cooler, take a left down the hallway and follow it around to the breakable wall. Bust through it and defeat the Alpha Missiles that stand guard in front of the generator room. Jump the missiles or punch them back at the launchers. Throw wall chunks or beat the snot out of them, then punch through the door to continue through the hallway. More Alpha Guards stand between the Hulk and the generator room. Use Sonic Claps to clear the hallway.

GENERATOR ROOM (I)

Inside the generator room are more Alpha Guards, a big chunk of wall, a picnic table, and computer terminals that hold regenerating Rage and Health power-ups. Destroy the generator to bring down the force field in the hallway to the right of the meat cooler. The generator itself breaks into a couple of pieces, one of which can be picked up and used as a weapon. Head back to the hallway and pass the meat cooler. In the hallway are two more Alpha Missiles.

OPTIONAL HALLWAY (J) AND ROOM (K)

The hallway to the left of the Alpha Missiles connects to an optional room (**K**). In this room are computer terminals that hold Continue, Health, and Rage power-ups. There is no reason to enter this room unless you need these items.

ROOM (L)

With the generator destroyed and the hallway force field down, enter Room (**L**). Inside this room are Alpha Shielders, computer terminals that hold Health and Rage power-ups, crates to smash the Shielders with, and two auto-guns at the rear of the room. One hit with a crate destroys an autogun. Move quickly to destroy the autoguns and Alpha Shielders. A healthy dose of Alpha Guards soon enters the room. Destroy the computer terminal on the right side of the room closest to the glass wall to pick up a Continue. The crate clos-est to this terminal contains a major Health power-up. Smash through the window in the back of the room and jump down to the connecting room below.

ROOM (M)

Two water pipes and many crates are in this room, and the only enemies are the ones who enter the room from the connecting hallway. Destroy the crates in the room to find Health and Rage power-ups. Once the coast is clear, break through the doorway and head into the hallway that the enemy used to enter the room.

HALLWAY (N)

Break through a couple of doorway walls and battle the Alpha Missiles and Guards who stand in the way of entering the final room (**O**). Collect all the Health and Rage power-ups from fallen guards and find the two Health power-ups in the hallway just before the final room. You must be in tip-top shape before stepping into the last room.

CHAMBER (O)

Upon entering the last room, four large Gamma Guards and a few Alpha Guards make a run at you. Gamma Guards are Alpha Guards who have been enhanced by the Gamma Power. Ravage has been through here and must have turned the Leader onto the stolen Gamma Orb. There are two autoguns in the back of the room. If you're lucky enough to enter Rage mode when you enter the room, one Super Sonic Clap takes out both guns and knocks away the riffraff. If that doesn't happen, punch through the crowd (try a fully charged jumping punch) and quickly eliminate the autoguns.

The support beams around the room can be knocked down and used as clubs, but taking the time to knock them down could cost health as everyone and everything in the room is attacking all-out. Draw the fight over to the support beams and the collateral damage should eventually knock the struts down.

SMASH

GRAPPLING WHEN SURROUNDED

WHEN BATTLING LARGE GROUPS OF BIG ENEMIES, SUCH AS THE GAMMA GUARDS, USING GRAPPLE ATTACKS SERIOUSLY DAMAGES THE VICTIM AND PREVENTS THE OTHER LARGE ENEMIES FROM ATTACKING. PERFORM A GAMMA SLAM QUICKLY AFTER GRABBING THE LARGE OPPONENT OR IT WILL SOON SHAKE FREE.

The crates along the back wall near the autoguns hide Health and Rage power-ups. Once the four Gamma Guards have been eliminated, multiple troops of Alpha Guards enter the room as others are being eliminated. Stay alive through the onslaught of Alpha Guards until two more Gamma Guards appear. Defeat these two and green arrows appear on the panel in the middle of the floor. When this happens, jump up and Gamma Stomp or throw a crate down on it to drop through the floor.

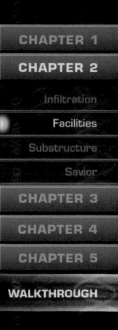

Ravage has used the power of the Orb to create Gamma-powered mutants to face the Hulk. Time is running out. Find Betty and the Orb.

GAMMA DOG CHAMBER (A)

From the beginning of the level Gamma Dogs attack, which seems appropriate in the middle of a chamber filled with Gamma Dog cages. After taking out the first beast, another takes its place. At most, you face three at a time. Defeat the Gamma Dogs using long combos and avoid jumping attacks. Break through the doorway and proceed to the connecting hallway.

HALLWAY (B)

Grab the broken piece of the doorway and take it to the end of the first hallway. Beat the Alpha Guards with the rock, then bust through the two walls. Continue to pick up wall fragments and squish the remaining guards before entering the next chamber (**C**).

CHAMBER (C)

Inside Chamber C is an encounter with four Gamma Guards and a choice of two exits. Defeat the Gamma Guards using grappling attacks, keeping the non-grabbed enemies from attacking. Break the columns and use stone chunks to crush the guards. When finished with the big blue guys, break down the door on the right side of the room and enter the following hallway (**D**).

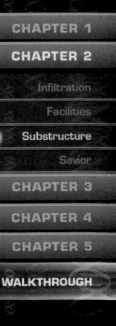

CHAPTER 1

CHAPTER 2

Infiltration

Facilities

Substructure

Savior

CHAPTER 3

CHAPTER 4

CHAPTER 5

WALKTHROUGH

HALLWAY (D)

Four more Gamma Guards wait in the hallway. Continue to use the wall chunks as often as possible. Two hits of a heavy wall piece takes out a Gamma Guard. If they surround you, revert to grappling moves. Bust through the door to the following arena sized room. A force field engages just behind the Hulk, preventing a return to the hallway. Enter the following room (**E**).

GENERATOR ARENA (E)

Around the perimeter of the large arena are four autoguns. In the middle of the room is the Generator that brings down the force field in the hallway just exited. The door to the left has a force field beyond it that is not shut down by destroying this generator. First, destroy the autogun closest to the entry point of the room. Take a barrel, run to the next autogun and destroy it. Continue around the room and try to get rid of the autoguns before the Gamma Guards drop into the room from the ledges above.

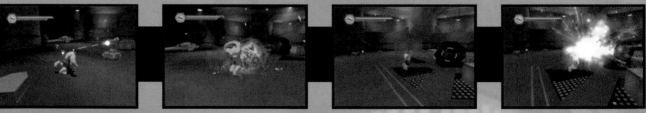

The large storage containers in the room make great Gamma Guard smashers! Beating the helicopter leaves a burnt out shell. Pick up this heavy shell and use it to beat the Guards. Throw a couple of the containers at the generator in the middle of the room. Avoid touching the generator; it shocks you, then knocks you off your feet the second time it's hit. More Gamma Guards enter the room after destroying the generator. Continue to smash them with the containers or leave the room through the door to Hallway (**D**).

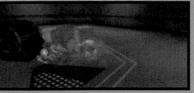

CHAMBER (C)

Head back to Chamber (**C**), defeating three more Gamma Guards that reappear in the hallway, then break down the other door inside the chamber to enter hallway (**F**).

HALLWAY (F)

Three Health power-ups, which appeared in the generator destruction cinematic, are located in this hallway. Defeat the two Gamma Guards and two Alpha Guards, then break down the following two doors. Grab a wall chunk before entering the next generator arena (**G**).

GENERATOR (G)

There are three generators in this arena. The generator on the left is guarded by one autogun, two auto-guns protect the one in the middle, and the generator on the right has three autoguns surrounding it. If the generator is destroyed, its autoguns retract and cease to fight (Health power-ups are left in their place). The room is initially devoid of enemies. Quickly eliminate the first generator with a thrown wall piece and a follow-up with the storage container to the left.

Pick up the shell of the broken generator and toss it at the middle generator. Destroy the helicopter and pick up the large shell. Three Gamma Guards attack at this time. Smash them with the shell or whatever else it takes to get rid of them. Find another storage container to throw at the middle generator to destroy it. Three more Gamma Guards attack, so deal with them. Use the generator shell and containers to squish them.

Gamma Guards continue to appear, so quickly take another container and begin attacking the last generator. When the last generator is destroyed, the force field in hallway (**H**) powers down. Bust through the doorway and enter the hallway.

HALLWAY (H)

Break through the walls, taking chunks of wall to defeat the few Alpha Guards and beat down upcoming walls. Break down the door to the following room (**I**) and enter it while holding a large chunk of wall.

ROOM (I)

Use the wall chunk and Grapple moves to defeat the three Gamma Guards in this small balcony-like room. The door on the far side of the room leads to the first arena (**E**), so don't head that way. Jump down to the lower room (**J**) and continue with the battle.

ROOM (J)

This is the final battle in this level. Defeat as many Alpha and Gamma Guards as you wish, but continue to pick up objects and throw them at the door along the back wall. Health power-ups can be found by breaking the computer terminals located around the perimeter of the room. Use the tables to hit the door in-between bouts with the enemy (use the Change Target button when necessary). As soon as the door is broken, a cinematic shows the Hulk leaving the room and heading toward the end of the level.

Madman has placed Betty Ross in the irradiation chamber. Destroy the computer consoles to disable the chamber and save Betty! Once the consoles are destroyed, defeat Madman!

Irradiation Chamber

THE MADMAN WAS ORIGINALLY PHIL STERNS, A FELLOW GRADUATE STUDENT OF BRUCE BANNER. HIS ADMIRATION FOR BRUCE TURNED TO JEALOUSY. ONCE HE LEARNED THAT DR. BANNER WAS THE HULK, STERNS DELIBERATELY EXPOSED HIMSELF TO AN EXCESS OF GAMMA RADIATION, EVENTUALLY GAINING THE POWERS OF MADMAN. NOW, AS MADMAN, HE IS OBSESSED WITH DESTROYING THE HULK.

MADMAN

MADMAN HAS BETTY IN AN IRRADIATION CHAMBER AND IS IN THE PROCESS OF ADMINISTERING DOSES OF RADIATION IN AN ATTEMPT TO MUTATE HER. YOU MUST SHUT DOWN THE CHAMBER BY SMASHING THE COMPUTERS BEFORE HER LIFE METER RUNS OUT OR ELSE THE MISSION IS FAILED.

BOSS ATTRIBUTES

MADMAN HAS THE ABILITY TO PERFORM HYPERDASH; THIS IS A SERIES OF MULTIPLE DASHING ATTACKS RECOGNIZABLE WHEN FLAMES SHOOT FROM MADMAN'S BODY AS HE SPRINGS FORWARD. AFTER SEVERAL DASHES, MADMAN IS VULNERABLE AS HE RECOVERS FROM THIS MOVE. NOT ONLY CAN HE QUICKLY CATCH UP TO YOU WITH THIS MOVE, IF HE HITS YOU, YOU ARE FLOORED. DASH OUT OF THE WAY TO AVOID THIS MOVE. THE QUICKEST REACTION TO THIS MOVE IS ALSO TO JUMP INTO THE AIR. THIS WORKS, BUT WHEN YOU LAND THERE'S A SLIGHT RECOVERY TIME LEAVING YOU VULNERABLE TO ATTACK. TO COUNTER THIS DRAWBACK TO THE JUMP, PERFORM A GAMMA STOMP BEFORE YOU LAND THE JUMP AND IF MADMAN IS CLOSE ENOUGH TO HIT YOU, HE WILL BE CAUGHT IN THE SHOCKWAVE! THIS WILL TEMPORARILY STUN HIM. THIS IS A GREAT TIME TO HIT HIM.

HE ALSO HAS THE ABILITY TO PERFORM A CHOKESLAM; THIS IS A GROUND-SLAMMING GRAPPLE ATTACK MUCH LIKE THE HULK'S GAMMA SLAM. THERE'S NO ESCAPING A GRAPPLE ATTACK, YOU JUST HAVE TO RIDE IT OUT. THE ONLY WAY TO AVOID IT IS TO KEEP YOUR DISTANCE, BUT IF YOU'RE USING GRAPPLE ATTACKS, THIS CAN'T BE DONE.

HIS ONLY OTHER UNIQUE ATTACK IS HIS OWN VERSION OF THE GAMMA STOMP; ONLY HE CAN PERFORM THIS MOVE FROM A STANDING POSITION AND WITH ONE LEG. THIS IS AN AIMED ATTACK AND A GOOD AMOUNT OF AREA IN FRONT OF HIM IS AFFECTED. YOU CAN SEE RED FLAMES SHOOT FROM THE GROUND IN THE AFFECTED AREA WHEN HIS GIANT FOOT REPEATEDLY BASHES THE FLOOR. HE ALSO POSSESSES THE ABILITY TO USE MANY OF THE SAME COMBOS THAT YOU HAVE ACCESS TO, MAKING HIM A FORMIDABLE OPPONENT.

THE BATTLE ENVIRONMENT

THE BATTLE ARENA IS A LARGE OVAL ROOM WITH THE IRRADIATION CHAMBER FILLING THE MIDDLE. THIS CHAMBER COMES IN HANDY FOR RUNNING FROM THE ENEMIES (RUN AROUND THE CHAMBER TO AVOID MISSILES AND CREATE DISTANCE BEFORE SETTING UP THE NEXT ATTACK). THERE ARE NO OBJECTS TO PICK UP TO USE AS WEAPONS OR TO DESTROY FOR HOPES OF HIDDEN POWER-UPS. THERE ARE TWO DOORS THAT ISSUE ALPHA AND GAMMA GUARDS DURING THE COURSE OF THE BATTLE. IF YOU LOOK AT THEM AS WALKING HEALTH AND RAGE POWER-UPS, THAT'S GOOD. IF YOU ALLOW THESE TROOPS TO GET THE BETTER OF YOU, IT'S BAD.

THE BATTLE

THIS IS A TWO-STAGE BATTLE. THE FIRST STAGE IS SPENT SAVING BETTY BEFORE HER LIFE METER EMPTIES. THE SECOND STAGE BEGINS AFTER SAVING BETTY AND DEFEATING MADMAN BECOMES THE PRIORITY. RUN TO THE OPPOSITE SIDE OF THE CHAMBER THAT MADMAN IS ON AND BEGIN DEMOLISHING THE

COMPUTER TERMINALS. HOPEFULLY YOU CAN TAKE ONE TERMINAL OUT BEFORE MADMAN IS ALL OVER YOU. RUN AROUND THE CHAMBER FROM HIM AND JUMP AWAY FROM HIS ATTACKS WHILE ENDING THE JUMP WITH A GAMMA STOMP. THIS STUNS MADMAN AND ALSO HELPS DAMAGE THE NEARBY COMPUTER TERMINALS. MADMAN OCCASIONALLY STOPS AND STARTS WORKING ON ONE OF THE COMPUTERS. AGAIN, HEAD TO THE OPPOSITE SIDE AND START BASHING A CONSOLE.

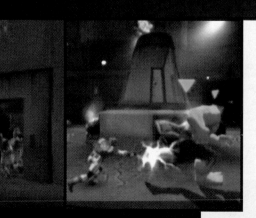

NOT LONG AFTER BASHING THE COMPUTERS, MADMAN'S FIRST WAVE OF BACKUP ARRIVES THROUGH ONE OF THE ELEVATOR DOORS. THE FIRST WAVE CONSISTS OF AN ALPHA MISSILE AND TWO ALPHA SHOCKERS. HIDING BEHIND THE COMPUTER FROM MISSILE ATTACKS PROVIDES PROTECTION AND FORCES THE ENEMY TO ASSIST IN TAKING CARE OF THE COMPUTERS. TAKE OUT THE TROOPS AS QUICKLY AS POSSIBLE AND RETURN TO DESTROYING THE CHAMBER COMPUTERS, OCCASIONALLY KEEPING AN EYE ON BETTY'S HEALTH METER. IF MADMAN WON'T LEAVE YOU ALONE, PICK HIM UP AND THROW HIM AT A COMPUTER. BETTER YET, TARGET AN OBJECT ON THE OUTSIDE OF THE ROOM AND TOSS HIM FAR AWAY.

ONCE ALL FOUR TERMINALS HAVE BEEN DESTROYED BETTY IS SAVED, BUT REMAINS IN THE CHAMBER AND MADMAN BECOMES FURIOUS. A CINEMATIC DEPICTS HIS TEMPER. HIS HEALTH METER REFILLS IN THE SECOND STAGE (WHICH IS THE REASON TO AVOID WASTING TIME TRYING TO BEAT HIM WHILE BETTY IS IN DANGER). NOW THE SECOND TASK BEGINS, AND THIS IS THE TOUGH PART—KEEPING ENOUGH HEALTH TO BEAT MADMAN AND LEADER'S HENCHMEN.

THE KEY TO DEFEATING MADMAN IS TO HIT HIM WHEN HE'S RECOVERING AFTER HIS COMBOS OR SPECIAL MOVES. DEFEAT HIS CRONIES WHEN HE IS NOT NEAR AND THRASH THEM FOR HEALTH AND RAGE POWER-UPS. THE SECOND WAVE OF BACK-UP (AND FROM HERE ON OUT) CONSISTS OF A GAMMA GUARD AND TWO ALPHA MISSILES. TAKE ADVANTAGE OF TIMES OF RAGE, AS EVERY ATTACK CAUSES DOUBLE DAMAGE.

IF YOU PLAN ON USING CHARGED JUMPING ATTACKS, MAKE SURE THERE ARE NO ALPHA MISSILES IN THE AREA. THEY PICK YOU RIGHT OUT OF THE SKY! THE BEST THING TO DO IS PERFORM GRAPPLING ATTACK AFTER GRAPPLING ATTACK. WHEN THE BACKUP ARRIVES, PICK UP MADMAN OR A GAMMA GUARD. FACE THE CLOSEST ENEMY AROUND AND SLAM YOUR CAPTIVE ONTO ANOTHER ENEMY. YOU MUST AIM QUICKLY OR THE CAPTIVE MAY WIGGLE FREE.

MADMAN

ONCE MADMAN IS BEATEN, BETTY EXITS THE CHAMBER AND ASKS HULK TO GET HER TO THE MILITARY GAMMA BASE TO FIND AN ANTIDOTE FOR HER EXPOSURE TO THE HULK'S GAMMA ILLNESS!

CRITICAL MASS

General Ryker is only too pleased to have you as his prize test subject. Incapable of transforming to the Hulk due to the gamma suppressing drugs in his system, Banner must first find an antidote and escape the subterranean Gamma Base. Be careful, the disguise will not hold up to close scrutiny.

PATROLLING SOLDIER	
SOLDIER	
SCIENTIST	
PATROL ROUTE	

CAPTURED!

As the Hulk delivers Betty Ross to the Military Gamma Base, the force field that surrounds the base is activated, trapping both Betty and the Hulk inside. General Ryker orders the dissection of Bruce Banner! Luckily, Betty escapes and frees Bruce from the operating table. She informs Bruce that the Leader is building a Gamma Army. It's time to escape and recover the Gamma Orb so the Hulk's essence cannot be used against anyone.

The soldier that Betty knocked out gives up his uniform that serves as a disguise. This disguise only works at a distance from other soldiers and scientists. If either spots you, doors are locked down and everyone in the area begins to attack. The sedatives block the ability to turn into the Hulk, so an antidote must be pieced together.

FLOOR 1

BLUE POTION

The first task is to get to chemical storage on level 5. The level begins just outside of the operating room (**A**). Follow the lighted tracks on the floor to the first security door. Walk up to the green button on the left and open the door. Just beyond the door (**B**) in the following tunnel are guards on patrol and some stationary guards near the security doors. There area also scientists walking around. Personnel on the move are the major risk in terms of being detected. When entering a new area, stop and scan the area (use the Free Look button) for soldiers and scientists to plot a route.

SECRET

CONTINUE & UCI

IF YOU CONTINUE HEADING DOWN THE MAIN TUNNEL WITHOUT HEADING FOR LIFT ROOM DOOR (C) YOU WILL FIND THE GUN RANGE ROOM AT THE END OF THE TUNNEL. INSIDE THE RANGE IS A CONTINUE ON THE LEFT SIDE OF THE ROOM AND A UNIVERSAL CODE INPUT TERMINAL. USE THE MAP TO PLOT YOUR ROUTE PAST THE PATROLLING GUARDS.

Hug the left wall and stop at the corner to allow the patrolling guard in the left tunnel move out of the way and then proceed to security door (**C**). Open the door and enter the following tunnel. Inside the following room are one stationary soldier guarding the lift ramp (**D**) and a patrolling guard. Wait for the patrolling guard to face the computer on the left wall and head up the lift ramp sticking to the walls to the right. Once on the circular lift (**E**), press the button on the back handrail computer to activate the lift and to access floor 5.

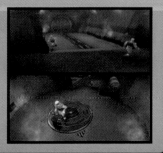

FLOOR 2: CHEMICAL STORAGE

There are two color potions on the second floor and it doesn't really matter which one you get first. To retrieve the blue potion first, head down the ramp from the lift (**F**) to the right and walk to the doorway (**G**) while avoiding the patrolling guards.

In the following tunnel, the route splits to the left and right. There's a potion at the end of each route. For now, take a right and head for door (**H**) while avoiding the walking scientists. Through the door is a curved tunnel with three scientists, one of which does not move at all. Walk around the scientists and head for the automatic glass door near the stationary soldier (**I**). The soldier is close, but you can get through the door without being caught. When you walk in front of the door, it will open.

CRUSH

SIDE ROOMS

THERE ARE SIDE ROOMS FILLED WITH COMPUTER SERVERS AND MANY OF THEM HOLD A POWER-UP OR TWO. THESE ROOMS ARE ALSO GOOD FOR HIDING FROM A PATROLLING GUARD OR FROM SOMEONE IN PURSUIT.

In the first lab [**J**], hug the left wall and follow it until you see the potion station with the green arrows pointing to the challenge console. Complete the challenge to receive the Blue Potion. The challenge is the same as the others only this time there are ten digits. If you don't finish the code in twenty seconds, try it again. Since the code is random, the challenge may be easier when you start again. Take the Blue Potion from the tray and head out of the lab the same way you entered. A blue potion icon now appears below your health meter.

SMASH
KNEE-TO-THE-GUT

WHEN PURSUED BY MULTIPLE SOLDIERS OR SCIENTISTS THE BEST FIGHTING MOVE AVAILABLE TO BANNER IS THE GRAPPLING ATTACK. WHEN NOT SNEAKING UP ON SOMEONE, IT BECOMES A KNEE TO THE GUT AND FLOORS OPPONENTS. THIS DOES PLENTY OF DAMAGE (FOR BANNER VALUES OF DAMAGE) AND THE ENEMY HAS TO RECOVER BACK TO HIS FEET. IN THIS TIME, YOU COULD EITHER FOCUS ON ANOTHER ENEMY OR RUN IN ATTEMPTS TO LOSE THE PURSUERS.

YELLOW POTION

Head back through doors [**I**] and [**H**] and head past the original hallway to the left continuing to the second lab through doors [**K**] and [**L**]. Stay mostly to the right wall of the tunnel to avoid being spotted. Just before automatic door [**L**] is a Continue in the small server room on the right side of the tunnel. Continue through the doors and head into the second lab [**M**]. In this lab, follow the left wall around the perimeter of the room until you spot the potion station near the back wall. The computer faces the back wall. Walk right up to it and crack the code challenge.

This challenge involves ten random digits with twenty seconds to complete it. Complete the challenge, take the Yellow Potion from the tray and exit the room the same way you entered. A yellow potion icon now appears below your health meter. Head back to the lift [**F**] and take it up to the next floor.

MIXING THE POTIONS

You now must mix the two potions using one machine, then use another machine to load a syringe with the antidote. As soon as you reach the top floor, head around the lift railings and run for the back of the room (don't head down the stairs). Find the nook to the right of the three windows overlooking a lab with a tank in the center. Find the dark shaded corner to the left of the tunnel (**O**) and wait there until four soldiers enter the room. Two soldiers stand on either side of the lift and remain there for some time. Two others patrol the room and one of these eventually heads downstairs. Move into the tunnel they exited as soon as the four of them pass by you. One guard heads back towards the tunnel to watch before moving to the stairs himself.

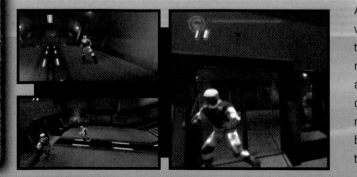

At this time, the drug starts taking effect and your vision becomes cloudy (rainbow clouds). Continue through the tunnel (which is clear of any enemies now) and head through automatic door (**P**). Again, a soldier stands guard near the door. If he sees you, dash inside the transition tunnel and hide in the nook near the automatic door and the soldier won't be able to open the door. Wait a while and his attention soon wanders to other things.

In the mixing lab (**Q**) are a tank, two soldiers, and four scientists. The tank has a force field that is engaged every five seconds and remains engaged for another five. If you run into or are hit by the force field you will be knocked off your feet, and the enemies begin attacking. The trick is to wait for the moment the tank shield is down and run along the left side of the room, staying close to the tank to avoid being spotted by the scientists on the computers to the left.

Head straight back for the potion mixing machine before the tank shield is engaged again. Bruce places the Blue Potion inside the machine and the Yellow Potion inside the tray. Walk over to the computer screen to the right and begin the familiar digit code challenge. Beat it and take the mixed antidote from the tray. A green antidote icon appears below your health meter.

The door that you entered the lab through is now locked and you must exit out of the other door (**R**). There are two soldiers near the door and more scientists on the other side of the room. It's best to allow the tank shield to activate, walk along the edge of the shield back the way you came and continue past the door you entered. Continue to follow the edge of the tank shield past the two soldiers and head out the door to the left of them (**R**).

FILLING THE SYRINGE

Through the following tunnel are four Health power-ups. These are here in case any health was lost due to skirmishes with guards. Go through the following door and walk to the far side of the consoles in the middle of the next lab (**S**). Place the antidote into the tray marked with glowing green arrows, then head to the computer screen to the right of the tray to work on the random digit code challenge. Once the challenge is completed, take the inoculating gun from the tray. You now have the antidote and a means to administer it! Go through the following door (**T**) to make your way back to the lift (**N**).

Tunnel (**U**) is full of soldiers. If you came through this tunnel instead of the upper tunnel when you first arrived on this floor, two scientists would be standing in the tunnel. These scientists are gone now and have been replaced by four stationary guards and two patrolling ones. Stick to the right wall of the tunnel the whole way through.

In the large room (**V**) is a Continue in nook to the right, more stationary soldiers in the distance and a patrolling guard. These are the guards that were first encountered upstairs when you entered this floor, meaning the floor above is clear. Avoid the patrolling guard and stick to the right side of the room. Follow the perimeter around until reaching the stairs. Head up the stairs and get onto the lift. When you do, a cinematic takes over to the end of this level.

Now cured of the gamma-depleting sedatives, the Hulk must escape Desert Base. Keep heading upwards until reaching the surface. The military uses every weapon they have to stop the escape and recapture their specimen.

ESCAPING THE BASE

As the elevator (**A**) reaches the next level of the base, three Shockshielders greet you with their batons and three others escape to the connecting tunnel.

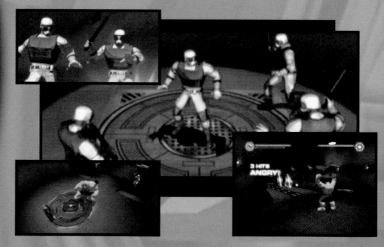

Run into the room and grab the spool-looking table and start beating the Shockshielders with it. Bash down the door (it's a thick metal one, so more force is required) and bash the pipes that line the side of the tunnel. Grab a pipe and start attacking the three newly arrived Shockshielders.

Inside the room to the left (**C**) are three Rifle Soldiers (if some haven't poured out into the tunnel when you were taking on the Shockshielders). Destroy the troops, then take out the three computers in the room to find a Continue and two Rage power-ups.

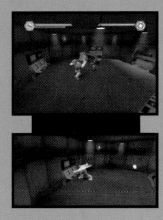

Take another pipe from the tunnel wall (one good punch should free a few from the wall) and bash down the door to the second sentry station (**D**). Inside are two Shockshielders and three unequipped Soldiers. Pick up the spool table and smash the Shockshielders first, then pound everyone! Smash the two computers for a Health and a Rage power-up.

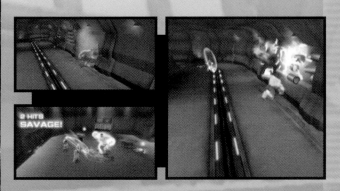

Bash down the door in the back of this sentry room to enter connecting tunnel. Again, three Shockshielders attempt to slow you down. Grab pipes from the walls and beat them senseless. Continue to the end of the tunnel and treat their pals with the same respect. Throwing the pipes at the Shockshielders takes them out with one hit! Enter the third sentry room (**F**) and defeat the soldiers inside. Smash the computers for three Rage power-ups. Break down the metal security door (**G**) and enter the next area.

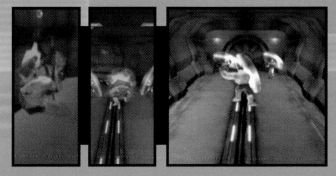

ROBOTS ATTACK!

Though door (**G**) are five soldiers, some with rifles some just wanting to punch you. Take them all out with Sonic Claps and proceed to the large lift. When you step foot into the "ring" (**H**), a series of Robots challenge you to a fight to the death (or deactivation as the case may be). These US Army mechanoids are designed to engage the Hulk head-on. They have enormous physical strength, classified A-class alloy construction with internal fusion generators.

In the first round you battle two Robots at a time. The next team of two Robots does not arrive until the first two are destroyed. Robots have a blue ray beam that they can shoot from their fists. This blue laser knocks you down, so run or jump and hold a charge attack to avoid this attack. The best way to defeat all the Robots, no matter how many are on you at once, is to use the Grapple move, then quickly face another Robot and toss one on top of the other, but not over the edge (they return at the top of the elevator, healed). Repeat this until all are defeated. When the second team of Robots has been dismantled, the lift rises to the next floor where more Robots and Soldiers attack. Take the Rifle Soldiers out first with Sonic Claps, then concentrate on the Robots. Head through the door (**I**) to access more tunnels.

RETURN TO THE TUNNELS

Run through the ends of the tunnel and pick up the two Rage power-ups, then jump or push past the Shockshielders to get at the pipes on the walls. Start pummeling the enemy with pipes and head to the end of the tunnel and pound down the next two doors (**J**).

ROBOT LABS

Inside the Robot lab are four Robots and two Rifle Soldiers (the unarmed soldier that you saw in the entry cinematic is running around as well). If you take out the unarmed soldier before he can activate the robots, your battle here is easier. If you didn't get the unarmed soldier in time, concentrate your attacks on the Robots and use the Grapple and Toss strategy until you enter Rage mode. Defeat the soldiers when you need more health. Destroy the computers in the room to find a Continue and four Rage power-ups.

CHAPTER 1

CHAPTER 2

CHAPTER 3

Chemical Effect

Spearpoint

Containment Failure

Guardian

CHAPTER 4

CHAPTER 5

WALKTHROUGH

Bash through the next two doors (**L**) to open the door to the next and very crowded Robot lab (**M**). There are two lab technicians (unarmed soldiers) and eight Robots! Just as in the previous room, take out the technicians to make this battle easier. If the robots are activated, remain in the small connecting hallway between labs and allow the robots to filter into the hallway. Use Grapple and Toss to bash two Robots at a time (staying safe from attacks when in the lift animation). You're vulnerable once the enemy is lifted, so toss it quickly before they wiggle free or you're struck.

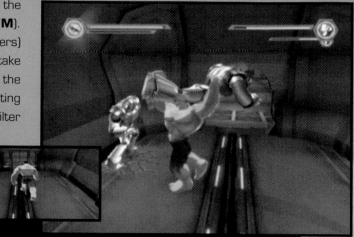

If it gets crowded in the hallway, back up into the first lab (**K**) and fight there. This thins the numbers and allows you to fight on your own terms. Jumping attacks allow the Robots to pick you out of the sky with their laser attack. Stick with Grapple attacks and long combos once you enter Rage mode.

RETURN TO THE TUNNELS

Once all eight Robots have been shutdown, head into the next hallway (**N**) through the breakable doors and defeat the three Shockshielders. Use the pipes on the walls to clear a path. Be aware that three more Shockshielders are waiting around the bend. Head to the T intersection and take the Rage power-up from the right tunnel and defeat the three Shockshielders and two Rifle Soldiers down the passageway to the left. Bust through the door (**O**) and be prepared to fight similar Robot battle as you push into the second lift room.

FIGHT FOR THE LIFT TICKET

This Robot battle is similar to the battle on the last lift, however this one is much tougher. Instead of just two teams of two Robots to defeat, you now go up against four different teams of varying amounts of Robots. Once you beat Team 4 and the lift takes you to the next level, four more Robots are waiting for you (Team 5).

Grapple and Toss remains the safest bet when fighting multiple enemies like this. Battle through the Rifle Soldiers and Shockshielders to reach the top floor door (**Q**).

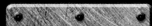

UNDERGROUND ENTRANCE

As you pass through the security door (**Q**), a barrage of Rifle Soldiers and Shockshielders begin to attack form the following room (**R**). Don't waste time with Sonic Claps, just run into the room and watch what happens. A huge gas explosion is triggered, large enough to take out all the humans. After recovering from the blast, pick up the Health left behind and prepare for the Robot drop. Four Robots jump into the room from somewhere above. Grab the large gas tanks and start bashing and throwing the lethal weapons at the mechanoids.

The explosion does massive amounts of damage to the Robots. Look for a Continue in one of the gas tanks along the back wall. After the initial four Robots are destroyed, five more drop into the room. After those five are blown up, six more appear. Try using a Sonic Clap when groups of Robots are around a gas tank, this makes a big scrap-metal mess. Upon approaching the door (**S**) after defeating the last group of six Robots, the mission ends.

Continues: 3

Continues: 3

CONTAINMENT

Having reached the surface, one more obstacle remains: Gamma Base's Energy Shield. Find a way to the source of the shield's power, destroy it and escape.

TANKS. YOU'RE WELCOME!

This is a fun, but short level. It can either be difficult or the easiest level so far, depending how you decide to play it. If you want to Hulk it up and destroy everything you see, then it could be a tough battle. If you just want to get out of the base and on with the story, then it's fairly easy.

The level begins inside the building where you destroyed all those Robots (**A**). Remember, the Hulk never passed through the metal door in the cinematic that ended the last level. The job now is to bash down this heavy metal door. It takes a bunch of punches to accomplish it. A cinematic plays as it takes its first good beating. In this cinematic, tanks roll in to try to stop the Hulk from leaving the base.

Once you break through the door, you find yourself on the outside looking down the barrels of three tanks! Now this is where you have options. Do you want it tough or easy? Having fun should be the answer.

HOW TO DESTROY A TANK

There are many different ways to take out a tank. Stand between two tanks and jump over the missiles to make the tanks shoot each other. Knock the missiles back at the tanks, but this is dangerous when there are multiple tanks. Throw large objects such as shipping containers, guard tower pieces, concrete, and large helicopter parts at the tank. If none of these things are on hand, try using soldiers as projectiles.

Run up to a tank before its shield engages, get in a good combo and dash away. Once one tank has been destroyed, use its pieces to throw at another tank. Each tank holds one major Health and four Rage power-ups. One grounded helicopter holds a major Rage power-up and the other holds a major Health power-up. If the Hulk enters Rage Mode while a missile is fired, it bounces off, just like anything else.

THE GREEN WAY

Continuing with the mean green way to beat this battle, keep in mind that many Rifle Soldiers attack as you progress through the base. Squash these guys with the many storage containers scattered about the area. Pound two or more soldiers at once with the container and take them out with one hit. These storage containers are most likely full of ammo and they explode impressively. Big boom. Throwing a container into a group of soldiers knocks them all on their backsides.

When you get past the first nine tanks and enter the pathway (**B**) just shy of the exit (**C**), four Robots attack. Keep the fight in the narrow pathway and away from the next three tanks around the corner. After taking out the four Robots, two more attack. Use the containers around the area to squash them. These heavy containers *really* bother them.

The last three tanks guard the entrance to the power core. Either take them on or run to the door (**C**) and suffer the damage as you beat the door down and end the level.

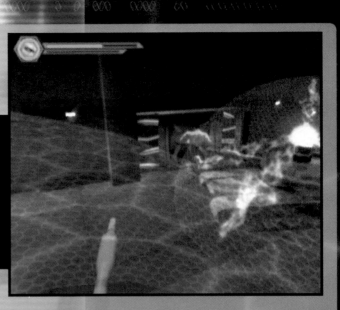

THE YELLOW WAY

Afraid of the big bad tanks? Well you're in luck. There is nothing stopping you from running all the way through the level from point (**A**) to point (**C**) without destroying anything except the final door. Just run around the tanks (they don't fire when the turret is turning and it turns to follow the Hulk's motion) and you can easily avoid missiles fired, if any are fired. Running ahead and not destroying anything has another advantage, there's no troop deployment. You won't see any soldiers along the way! When you reach the Robot ambush (**B**), just run by them. Head around the final corner with the three tanks and bash the door (**C**) in and end the level with ease.

GUARDIAN

After breaking through to the power core of the shield generator, find a way to use the generator mechanism to damage Flux. Defeat Flux to destroy the generator and escape Desert Base.

FLUX, A.K.A. PFC BENNY TIBBITS, WAS ENDOWED WITH UNSTABLE HULK-LIKE POWERS THROUGH SECRET MILITARY RESEARCH. HIS SUPERIOR OFFICER, GENERAL RYKER, HAS SUPPLIED THE ONLY INFORMATION FLUX HAS ON THIS PROCESS. HE IS COMPLETELY FAITHFUL TO RYKER AND IS DRIVEN BY A MISTAKEN BELIEF THAT DR. BANNER IS A FELON AND A TRAITOR TO HIS COUNTRY.

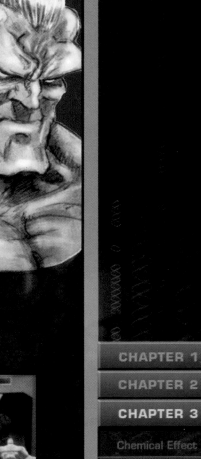

FLUX

BOSS ATTRIBUTES

THIS GAMMA ALTERED G.I. GOES BEYOND A LITTLE NUTS, HE'S COMPLETELY PSYCHOTIC! WAIT UNTIL YOU SEE HOW CARELESS HE IS WITH EXPLOSIVES. AS FLUX CHASES YOU AROUND THE ARENA, HE TOSSES GRENADES AND SOMETIMES RUNS IN TO THE HOT ZONE. FLUX SYSTEMATICALLY LEAPS ONTO THE UPPER BALCONY AND TOSSES DOWN GRENADES, SOME OF WHICH EXPLODE ON IMPACT.

HIS MOST IMPRESSIVE MOVE IS FISTS OF FURY. THIS IS A RAPID AND BLINDING SERIES OF GUT PUNCHES FOLLOWED BY A MASSIVE RIGHT HOOK, AND ENDS WITH BACKWARDS ROLL. THIS IS SIMILAR TO A GRAPPLE ATTACK AND YOU CANNOT INTERRUPT THIS ATTACK.

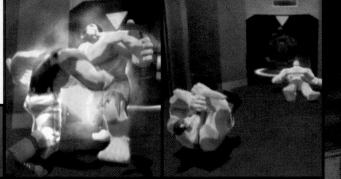

IN ANOTHER GRAPPLE-STYLE ATTACK, HE THROWS HIS KNEE IN TO YOUR GUT AND GIVES YOU A MASSIVE RIGHT-HANDED BACKHAND TO THE BACK OF THE NECK. THIS GUY DOESN'T MESS AROUND.

FINALLY, THE STRAIGHT-LEG KICK CONSISTS OF HIS LEG LASHING OUT AND LOCKING IN YOUR GUT. OUCH! IT KNOCKS YOU BACK WITH A BRILLIANT, GLOWING RED IMPACT. FLUX'S MILITARY EXPERIENCE HAS MADE HIM VERY RESILIENT TO HAND-TO-HAND COMBAT. YOU MUST FIND A MORE RESOURCEFUL WAY TO DEPLETE HIS HEALTH.

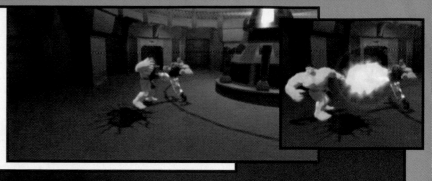

THE BATTLE ENVIRONMENT

THE BATTLE ARENA IS A ROUND CHAMBER THAT HOUSES A SHIELD CORE THAT GENERATES THE ENERGY NEEDED TO KEEP THE FORCE SHIELD AROUND THE BASE UP AND RUNNING. THERE ARE THREE ALCOVES THAT HOLD POWER CELLS. THESE POWER CELLS SUPPLY POWER TO THE FORCE FIELD THAT SURROUNDS THE SHIELD CORE. THERE'S A BALCONY THAT ENCOMPASSES HALF OF THE ARENA. FLUX LIKES TO JUMP UP THERE AND TOSS GRENADES DOWN. THERE'S NO WAY TO ACCESS THIS BALCONY. MAJOR HEALTH POWER-UPS APPEAR ON THE FLOOR WHEN FLUX LEAPS TO THE BALCONY. LOOK FOR THE THREE POWER-UPS NEAR THE THREE POWER CELLS. GRAB THEM FAST! THEY FADE AWAY WHEN FLUX RETURNS TO THE FLOOR.

THE BATTLE

BEING THAT FLUX IS SUPER-RESILIENT TO HULK BEATINGS, YOU MUST FIND A DIFFERENT WAY OF WEARING DOWN HIS HEALTH OR THE BATTLE LAST LONGER THAN IT SHOULD. THE ANSWER IS THE SHIELD CORE.

THERE ARE THREE STAGES INVOLVED IN THE PROCESS OF THROWING FLUX INTO THE SHIELD CORE. FIRST, DESTROY THE THREE POWER CELLS IN THE ALCOVES AROUND THE ARENA. ONCE THEY ARE DESTROYED, THE FORCE FIELD AROUND THE SHIELD CORE GOES DOWN.

SECOND, PICK UP FLUX WITH A GRAPPLE MOVE AND CARRY HIM SOMEWHAT CLOSE TO THE SHIELD CORE, THEN THROW HIM INTO IT. THIS BURNS MORE THAN A QUARTER OF HIS HEALTH!

3 HITS
ANGRY!

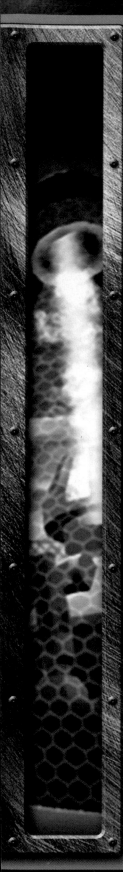

FINALLY, AFTER FLUX GETS FRIED, HE TAKES TO THE UPPER BALCONY AND TOSSES GRENADES. YOU COULD EASILY AVOID THIS ATTACK BY RETREATING TO THE OPPOSITE SIDE OF THE ROOM WHERE THE BALCONY AND HIS GRENADES DON'T REACH, BUT THE ONLY WAY TO GAIN HEALTH IN THIS BATTLE IS BY RETRIEVING THE HEALTH POWER-UPS THAT APPEAR BELOW THE BALCONY. ONCE THIS IS DONE, HE JUMPS BACK DOWN TO THE FLOOR AND THE PROCESS BEGINS ALL OVER AGAIN.

FLUX

NEVERTHELESS, THINGS DON'T ALWAYS GO AS PLANNED. FLUX WON'T JUST LET YOU DO ALL THIS WITHOUT A FIGHT. HE IS CONSTANTLY AT YOUR HEELS. KEEP YOUR FOCUS ON THE POWER CELLS. WHEN FLUX NEARS, HIT HIM WITH A LONG COMBO THAT KNOCKS HIM DOWN. AS SOON AS HE'S SAILING THROUGH THE AIR, TURN YOUR FOCUS BACK TO THE POWER CELL'S DESTRUCTION. USE RIGHT JABS OR AN OVERHEAD SMASH COMBO ON THE POWER CELLS. FLUX'S MIS-AIMED GRENADES OFTEN HELP IN THEIR DESTRUCTION. JUST BE SURE TO CLEAR THE AREA WHEN A GRENADE IS THROWN AT YOUR FEET.

THERE ARE TWO STAGES TO THE FLUX BATTLE. WHEN YOU HAVE COMPLETELY DEPLETED HIS HEALTH ONCE, FLUX BECOMES FIRE FLUX AND HIS HEALTH IS FULLY RESTORED. ALTHOUGH HE LOOKS MORE OMINOUS, HIS ATTACKS AND ROUTINE REMAIN THE SAME. REMEMBER THAT YOUR KICKS AND PUNCHES DO HARM HIM A LITTLE, SO IF HE HAS JUST A LITTLE HEALTH REMAINING BEFORE HIS TRANSFORMATION OR IF HE IS CLOSE TO COMPLETE ANNIHILATION, DON'T WASTE TIME WITH THE SHIELD CORE.

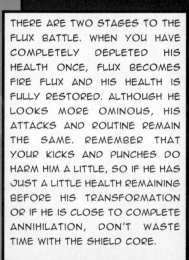

Return to Alcatraz, where the Leader is twisting the Hulk's energy to create a mutant army. Return to the underground facilities and pick up the trail of the Orb.

BREAKING BACK IN TO ALCATRAZ

This level opens in the Alcatraz compound [**A**] with the Hulk trying to gain entry. The creation of an entrance is quickly solved as a Gamma Elite comes barreling through a nearby door. The Gamma Elite are Gamma irradiated Alpha Guards and are the Leader's crack troops. They are equipped with large, powerful energy weapons designed specifically to affect Gamma creatures.

Following the Gamma Elite are five Alpha Guards. Use the large containers, barrels, girders, or crumbled storage house pieces to defeat Leader's troops. If you don't head into the hole created by the Gamma Elite soon, a steady flow of Gamma Guards and Alpha Guards will continue to pour into the compound.

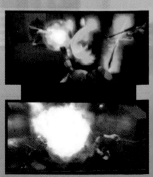

INSIDE ALCATRAZ

Once inside the prison, four Alpha Guards guard the L-shaped hallway. Take them out and punch the control panel (**B**) on the wall in the corner of the "L" to bring down the hallway force field. With that done, punch through the following door and enter the next passageway. Grab a girder from the hallway before entering the broken doorway.

GAMMA DOGS! (C)

With girder in hand, begin swinging at the Alpha Shielders and the Gamma Dogs in the new passageway (**C**). When the girder disintegrates, choose from the other array of items: a crate, more girders, and three explosive barrels. At the back of the passageway is a three-sectioned wall. Break through one of the sections and jump down to the recreation yard.

RECREATION YARD (D)

Jump down into the recreation yard (**D**). Two Gamma Elite guards follow out of the passageway. Avoid their fire while running to retrieve explosive barrels. Throw the barrels at the Elite before turning to battle the two Alpha Shielders and two Alpha Guards who were already in the yard. Reinforcements arrive through the holes in the wall above the yard. Either stick around to continue a lengthy battle against the same class troops, or, during a lull, break down the fence and jump to the lower yard (**E**).

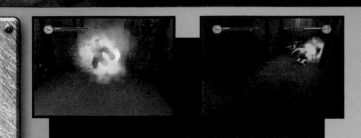

In the lower yard are metal planks, fence pieces, barrels, and a storage house that can used as weapons. The two Gamma Dogs should be dealt with, and more Gamma Guards follow from the upper yard. Fight until another pause in the flow of battle occurs, then break down the door and reenter the prison.

JAILHOUSE ROCK (F)

Inside the L-shaped hallway (**F**) is one locked and loaded Gamma Elite guard. If your friends from outside followed you into the hallway, try to defeat them at the broken door opening before rounding the corner and dealing with the armed Gamma freak. Use the crates in the corner to sandwich the enemy, then break through the following doorway. If health is needed, return to the yard and wait for a slow trickle of Alpha Guards to attack.

GAMMA DOG PENS (G)

Seems that all they lockup in Alcatraz nowadays is Gamma Dogs! As you enter the jail cell (**G**), a cutscene shows a force field protected exit and a couple hungry Gamma Dogs. To assist you in the dogfight are a girder, a large crate, and an explosive barrel. When all is said and done, five Gamma Dogs are released and you're stuck in a room with a force field that's still active. Pick up one of the objects in the room and target the steel covered control panel above the force field. Throw the object at it and the force field dies out, revealing a breakable door. Bust through and enter the next area.

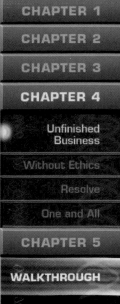

L-SHAPED HALLWAY (H)

Similar to the last L-shaped hallway, this one also has a control panel and a force field protecting the doorway. Smash the panel to shut down the force field. Bust through the breakable door before the Gamma Guard enters the hallway from the Jail Cell. Use the crate in the corner over his head if you do not escape his advance.

JAIL CELL 2 (I)

Another attack of Gamma Dogs occurs in the second jail cell (**I**). This time there are three at the start and three follow after their destruction. Smash one of the fuse panels on the walls to shut down the force field in the following hallway (**J**). Use the girders in the room to batter the mutts.

L-SHAPED HALLWAY (J)

Pick up the wall shard on the floor while passing into the L-shaped hallway (**J**). Round the corner and begin batting the two Gamma Elite guards. Two of these gun-wielding maniacs in a narrow area equals a bad situation. Try to pummel them with objects from the previous room or grab and throw one into the other. Don't try charged jump attacks, unless you enjoy being the clay pigeon for skeet shooters.

GAMMA AMBUSH! (K)

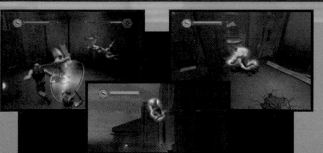

In the final room before you head outside again is an ambush by three Gamma Guards and two Alpha Shielders. Luckily, the room holds girders and explosive barrels. Clear a route to the 3-sectioned back wall quickly or face the onslaught of Gamma Guards and Alpha Shielders that spill into the room from the L-shaped hallway. Break through the wall and jump down into the courtyard.

COURTYARD (L)

As soon as you jump down into the courtyard, grab a barrel from a corner and start bashing one of the two Gamma Elite. If possible, knock them or throw them over the edge to the lower platform. The longer you remain on the upper courtyard area the more backup soldiers jump out of the building overhead. Create a lull in the fighting by defeating everyone in sight, then grab the regenerating barrels from around the building and start targeting and hurling them over the edge at the enemy on the lower platform.

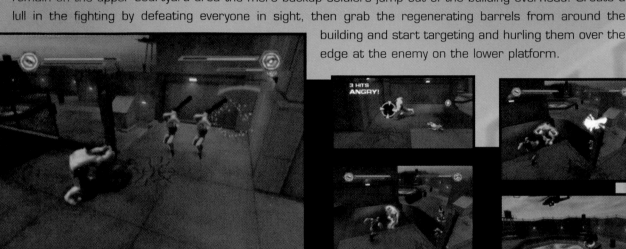

CHOPPER LAUNCH CHUTE (M)

Jump down to the lower platform and defeat the Shockshielders and Gamma Guards. They continue to generate in this area so quickly get on with the next task. Head to the back of the courtyard for the large hole in the ground. Out of the hole comes a helicopter. Pick up a barrel from around the hole and throw it at the chopper. It takes two explosive barrels to destroy one helicopter, and if you use other objects from around the hole it could take longer. When that helicopter is destroyed, another is deployed. You are under constant attack from the spawning Gamma Guards and Gamma Dogs, so you must balance your attacks against both the grounded and flying enemies. After eliminating three helicopters, the hole remains open. Jump through it to access the large hangar below.

CHOPPER HANGAR (N)

Jump down into the hangar (never saw this on the Alcatraz tour!) and head for the collection of storage containers. These things are huge and squish the Gamma Elite, Guard, Gamma Dog, and Alpha Guards like bugs under a shoe. However, the more you squish the more that arrive as replacements. The containers and barrels reveal Rage and Health power-ups when destroyed. Rush into the hallway (O) and into the room they have been spawning from (P).

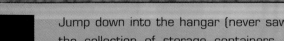

SWITCH ROOM (P)

The only enemies on narrow ledge are the ones that follow from the hangar. The longer you stand around, the more that pour in from that room. Jump down to the lower switch room area and destroy the three fuse panels on the walls (2 on the left wall, 1 on the right). Destroying the fuse panels shuts down the force field to the connecting hallway. On this lower switch room floor, Gamma Elite, Guards, and Alpha Guards regenerate. You need to get into the following hallway quickly. In the hallway (**Q**) are another two fuse panels, another force field, and a Gamma Elite. Quickly, knock the Elite down and destroy the fuse panels to bring down the force field so you can enter the irradiation chamber.

CRUSH

UPPER LEDGE HALLWAY FORCEFIELD

THE FORCE FIELD PROTECTING THE SHORT HALLWAY ON THE UPPER LEVEL OF THE SWITCH ROOM (P) DOES NOT SHUT-DOWN NO MATTER WHAT FUSE PANEL YOU SHUTDOWN. DON'T WASTE TIME OR HEALTH TRYING TO THROW BARRELS AT THE SWITCHES ON THE FIRST FLOOR TO GET THIS FORCE FIELD TO CLEAR. THE HALLWAY OBVIOUSLY LEADS OUTSIDE, AS YOU CAN SEE THE ORANGEY SKY.

IRRADIATION CHAMBER (R)

Remember this room? This is where you battled to save Betty Ross's life. Inside are Gamma Dogs, Alpha Guards, and a Gamma Guard. Lay down some green power on any of the enemies while more of the same arrive via the elevators in the back of the room. There are plenty of regenerating explosive barrels in this room to use against these enemies. Survive the mayhem and approach the double doors between the elevators and they open. However, four Gamma Elite enter the room through these doors. Stick around to defeat them or push past them and run through the last hallway (**S**) to complete the level.

WITHOUT ETHICS

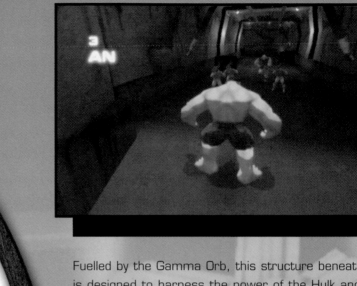

Fuelled by the Gamma Orb, this structure beneath Alcatraz is designed to harness the power of the Hulk and create a mutant army with it. Find the Gamma Orb and put an end to this plan.

SUBTERRANEAN TUNNELS (A)

The quest through the subterranean tunnels is a long one, but many of the lairs, battles, and enemies are the much the same. This is the lair of the Leader's Gamma army! It begins in the tunnel entered from the last level (**A**). The welcoming committee consists of three Alpha Guards and a Gamma Elite. Around the corner is a constant barrage of Alpha Guards and Missiles brings up the rear. Use Sonic Clap on large groups of puny soldiers. Push forward through the troops until reaching a breakable barrier, a door too small for the Hulk.

GAMMA ELITE (B)

Carry a barrel while rounding the corner to the barrier. Throw the barrel at the breakable wall and back up to grab more barrels. Retreat to the previous tunnel and allow the Elite to follow. This provides the necessary room to throw barrels at them. If they get too close, smash them before hurling the barrels away. In this level, never be too proud to retreat. There are many battles like this one where powerful enemies seem overwhelming.

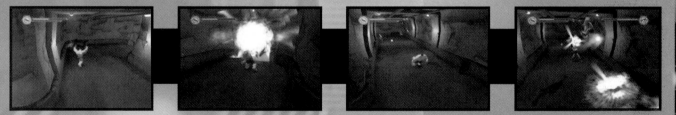

THE LAVISH TUNNEL (C)

Notice the difference in the tunnel walls (**C**) while entering the tunnel through the newly opened wall. They look as if someone was trying to make the place livable! There's a doorway (**O**) behind the Hulk with a force field beyond it, and another further around the bend (**D**). The door must wait until the force field is shut down. Break down door (**D**) and continue through the tunnel system.

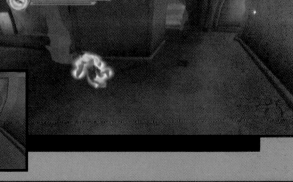

BACK TO THE ECONOMICAL TUNNELS (E)

A return to the crude looking tunnels brings barrels, support struts, and Gamma enemies. Fight through the two Gamma Dogs and two Alpha Missiles and blow down the next wall barrier. Beyond the opening is another tunnel system where the walls look finished (**F**).

THE OTHER LAVISH TUNNEL (F)

Along the right wall is another passageway blocked by a force field. Ahead is another breakable doorway barrier. Come back to passageway (**N**) when the force field has been shut down. Break through the wall and continue into the tunnel while holding a large wall chunk.

RETURN TO THE COST-CONSCIOUS TUNNELS (G)

Use the wall chunk to destroy the autogun (**G**) that protects the lair beyond it. Before entering the lair (**H**), break off a wall support from the tunnel for protection against encounters in the upcoming Gamma Guard's Lair.

LAIRS OF THE GAMMA GUARDS (H), (I), (J), (K)

Inside are five capsules with one Gamma Guard inside each. All but two of them burst open with an emerging guard. Use the two pieces of the autogun, the large gas tanks just inside the room to the left, or the tunnel supports as weapons. Destroying a capsule with a guard inside damages that guard when he comes out, making it easier to eliminate.

Continue through the lairs of the Gamma Guards (**H** through **K**) and draw the enemies out into the previous connecting tunnel to fight. Look for the barrel near the entrance of Lair (**J**) that contains a Continue. Many of the explosive barrels and gas tanks contain power-ups.

CRUSH

FORCE FIELD LAIR

TRYING TO RUN THROUGH THE LEVEL TO GET AS FAR AS POSSIBLE WITHOUT ENGAGING IN TOO MANY BATTLES? YOU MUST FINISH THE FIGHT IN LAIR (I) TO GET THROUGH THE FOLLOWING TUNNEL AS A FORCE FIELD IS PRESENT AT THE LAIR'S EXIT. BEAT THE GAMMA GUARDS FROM THIS LAIR TO SHUTDOWN THE FORCE FIELD.

GENERATOR PUZZLE (L)

Bust through the door and enter the force field generator room (**L**). Upon entering this room, two Gamma Dogs, two Alpha Guards, and a Gamma Elite spring an ambush from behind. Others of their type back them up when they are defeated. Begin punching the four large push-switches on the side of the generator until the blue lights turn red. If possible, fight around the switches as they take damage during the fight. Once all switches have been punched into the center of the generator, the force fields passed earlier (**N** and **O**) are shut down.

Head into the new passageway (**N**) and look for the very small door that appears to be a mouse hole in the baseboard (**M**). Just big enough for Bruce Banner to fit through, it doesn't come in to play in this level. For now, continue back to the original lavish tunnel to enter tunnel (**O**), which is not open. Alpha Guards appear along the way, but Sonic Claps and explosive barrels should take care of them.

NEW TUNNEL OPENING (O)

The newly opened tunnel (**O**) is a tough battle. Inside are many Gamma Dogs, Gamma Elite, and Alpha Guards. Again, the best strategy is to lure them into the previous tunnels and grab explosive barrels on the way. When there's enough room, throw the barrel. This tactic thins out the aggressors and provides more room in which to work. Take advantage of any rages by charging crowds and executing a Super Sonic Clap or Super Overhand Smash. Continue to charge and retreat until the area is clear. If health beyond what defeated enemies drop is needed, retreat and smash barrels. Most of them have Health and Rage power-ups.

CLIFF'S EDGE (P)

When the tunnel (**O**) is clear, head out and onto the ledge looking over the large chasm. A cutscene begins and in it, an Alpha Guard teases the Hulk into a trap. As the Hulk approaches the guard, the ledge explodes and he is thrown to the bottom of the deep cavern.

GAMMA DOG DEN (Q)

At the bottom of the large cavern, walk to the stalagmite with the green arrows. Break the stalagmite for a major Health power-up, then jump up onto the broken stump and again to the first ledge of the cliff. Destroy the autoguns (missile shooters) before the Gamma Dogs run down the cliff side to attack. Keep jumping up the ledges of the cliff side while battling Gamma Dogs until reaching the top.

Either stay and defeat all the Gamma Dogs, or avoid the dogs and concentrate on scaling the cliff. The dogs that jump down cannot jump up to the next tier, so there will always be around six Gamma Dogs to avoid on the way up. Avoid is the dogfight that ensues if you stay on the bottom floor of the cavern. A massive pack of Gamma Dogs will have the Hulk for dinner, so find all the low ledges that can be reached with a jump and get to moving. On one of the last ledges is another stalagmite that must be broken to use as a step. Inside the stalagmite is a Health power-up. Once on the top of the cliff, head to the right and enter the tunnel (**R**).

SMASH

HIGH-JUMP TIP

IF YOU HAVE TROUBLE JUMPING UP ON SOME OF THE HIGH LEDGES, PERFORM A CHARGED GAMMA CRUSHER, A JUMP ATTACK. THIS ALLOWS YOU TO GET MORE AIR AND SHOOTS THE HULK FORWARD AS THE ATTACK IS RELEASED.

FINAL TUNNEL (R)

Fight through the four Gamma Elite and Alpha Guards in the last tunnel, or just run ahead to the end of the tunnel (**S**) and finish the level. At the end of a tunnel, another booby trap has been rigged. A large bomb has been placed next to explosive barrels at the mouth of the tunnel.

CHAPTER 1

CHAPTER 2

CHAPTER 3

CHAPTER 4

Unfinished Business

Without Ethics

Resolve

One and All

CHAPTER 5

WALKTHROUGH

The energy blast and the transformation back to Bruce Banner saps Bruce's energy and he is temporarily incapable of transforming back into the Hulk. Find a safe way to move deeper into the complex and pursue the Gamma Orb.

THE BRUCE TRUCE

There's no getting the Hulk to help out here. This level is all about stealth and the element of surprise. The generator that was shut down in the previous level (to take down the force fields) also supplied power to the trolley (**C**). The trolley is the ticket out of the subterranean Alcatraz base. You must head back to that same generator and turn it back on.

The level begins in a rubble-filled cave with an exit filled with large boulders and live wires. Crouch and walk through the opening in the bottom of the boulders and exit the tunnel.

SLEEPING GAMMA DOGS

Continue crouching and walking while progressing toward the sleeping Gamma Dogs near the trolley car and stacks of crates. There are two routes available to get past the sleeping Gamma Dogs. Both require crouching while walking. Either head along the edge next to the trolley (**C**), continuing to sneak past the dogs to the next tunnel.

Or, move the brown crates inward into the circle of storage containers (**B**) and walk behind them to the following movable brown crates. Pull them back and creep past the dogs and into the tunnel behind them (**D**).

REENTERING THE TUNNELS

Once past the dogs and under the second rubble covered tunnel entrance (**D**), walk to the back of the tunnel and a cutscene takes Banner through the small doorway between the two gas tanks (**E**) and into tunnel system.

RETURNING POWER TO THE TROLLEY

Back in the tunnel system previously visited as the Hulk, head out of the baseboard hole (**E**) and take a right in the next room. Crouch and walk under the rubble filled doorway (**F**) and hug the right wall in the following tunnel. Hide behind the rock column (**G**) to avoid detection from the two guards up ahead. Wait in this spot until the roof caves in on the two guards.

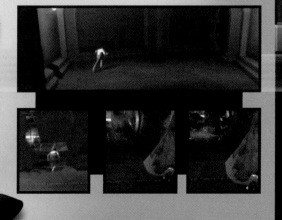

Head into the first Gamma Guard Lair and walk up to the capsule (**H**) near the exit and a short cutscene of Bruce's thoughts plays. Move into the following tunnel and stop just as after rounding the bend and wait for the ceiling (**I**) to fall before moving through into the following lair (**J**).

GAMMA DOG VS. ALPHA GUARDS

In the second Lair (**J**), a fight ensues between one Gamma Dog and two Alpha Guards. As the fight occurs and the participants are preoccupied, head into the room and hide behind one of the gas tanks in the room. The Gamma Dog takes out one guard and the remaining guard blows away the Gamma Dog. This leaves one enemy to get around. Creep along wall furthest from the direction he faces, sneak up to him and get him in a chokehold. Use the capsule to the right of the tunnel entrance he stands near as cover if necessary.

THE THIRD LAIR AND FALLING ROCKS

Continue through the tunnel to the third lair (**K**) and into the following tunnel. Stop short of entering the wider section of the tunnel (**L**) to allow the ceiling to fall in. Major damage is inflicted when hit by these huge falling rocks. Stop just before the tunnel narrows before the fourth lair, as the ceiling falls onto a gas tank (**M**). Double the trouble!

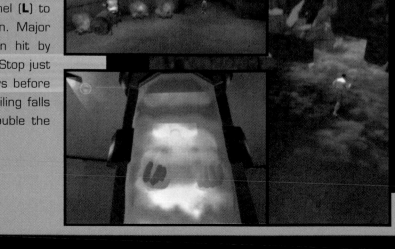

SLEEPY GAMMA DOGS

In the last lair (**N**) are three sleeping Gamma Dogs. Begin creeping from the entrance to the lair and continue to move silently between the two dogs on the right and the one on the left near the tunnel entrance. You really don't want to disturb their sleep. Mission failure is guaranteed if you do. Another quick cutscene dives into Bruce's conscious while passing the Gamma Guard capsule (**O**) near the lair exit. Run through the following tunnel and duck under the collapsed entrance to the generator room (**P**).

GENERATOR ROOM

In the generator room (**P**), push the four red buttons around the generator. Once all the red buttons have turned blue, the power is restored. Leave the room through the following exit (**Q**). The rocks blocking the exit explode and destroy the force field. Head into the hallway and follow the green arrows (**E**) back into the small hole.

GAMMA DOGS VS. BRUCE BANNER

The last task is the toughest challenge in this level. After leaving the small hole and reentering the tunnel, the Gamma Dogs that were asleep near the Trolley are up and on the move. Slowly approach the exit (**D**) after seeing the pack moving away to the left. Approaching the exit too soon makes it easy for the Gamma Dogs to spot you, and they won't move from this exit. Once they have moved to the left near the trolley, crouch and walk out of the tunnel and head behind the wall of containers. If you didn't use this route on the way into the tunnels you must move the brown crates to get behind the containers.

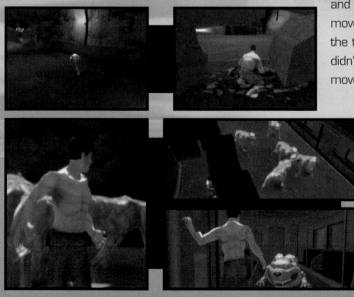

Move through the containers to the movable crates (**B**) and pull the right stack out of the way. Quickly dash out from behind the containers and make a beeline for the trolley's open door (**C**). Watch the Gamma Dogs, and as soon as a clearing is in sight, run for it! Reach the area in front of the trolley entrance and a cutscene takes over. Inside the trolley, Bruce discovers he is not alone.

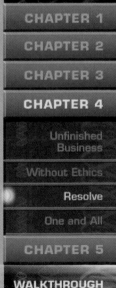

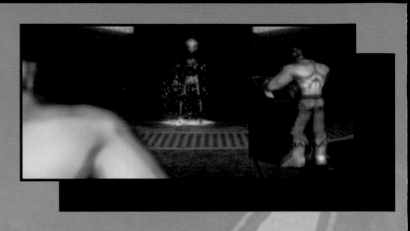

You've reached the teleportation device used to transport the Leader's army from Freehold. Defeat Ravage and follow the trail to the Gamma Orb.

A

B

C

D

E

RAVAGE

PROFESSOR CRAWFORD IS A BRILLIANT SCIENTIST AND RESEARCHER, AND BRUCE BANNER WAS HIS BEST STUDENT. CRAWFORD IS NOW A SICKLY MAN, LIVING OUT HIS TWILIGHT YEARS FROM THE CONFINES OF A WHEELCHAIR. EMBITTERED BY HIS CONDITION, PROFESSOR CRAWFORD IS OBSESSED WITH REGAINING HIS HEALTH AT ANY COST. HE FOUND THAT MANIPULATING GAMMA POWER ALLOWS HIM TO TURN INTO A FORM HE CALLS "RAVAGE," A HULK-LIKE MONSTER. IN RAVAGE FORM HE EXHIBITS HULK-CLASS STRENGTH AND SIMILAR ABILITIES.

BOSS ATTRIBUTES

RAVAGE HAS THE ABILITY TO USE ALL THE SAME BASIC FIGHTING MOVES AS THE HULK. HE PERFORMS FAMILIAR COMBOS AND JUMP ATTACKS SUCH AS THE CHARGED RIGHT HOOK AND THE GAMMA CRUSHER. HE'S BEEN STUDYING THE HULK, HE KNOWS HIM, AND HE WANTS TO BE DONE WITH THE HULK ONCE AND FOR ALL.

THE BATTLE ENVIRONMENT

THE ARENA IS A LARGE CAVERN WITH A TELEPORTER AT THE FAR END. THE EXPLOSION THAT ROCKED THE BASE HAS CREATED A SHAKY FOUNDATION AND ANY JOLT SENDS PIECES OF THE ROCKY CEILING CRASHING TO THE FLOOR. THE CENTER OCTAGONAL AREA OF THE ARENA IS THE SAFEST AREA FROM FALLING ROCKS, MAKING THE OUTER LYING AREAS THE MOST SENSITIVE TO AVALANCHES.

THE BATTLE

THROW THE DEAD GAMMA DOG OFF THE TROLLEY AND EXIT TO THE LEDGE (A). HEAD TO THE END OF THE LEDGE (B) NEAR THE TUNNEL ENTRANCE (C) AND PERFORM A GAMMA STOMP. QUICKLY MOVE OUT OF THE FALLING DEBRIS AND WAIT FOR A STONE CLUB TO LAND. PICK UP THE CLUB AND MOVE INTO THE BATTLE ARENA (D) THROUGH THE SHORT TUNNEL (C).

INSIDE THE CAVERN, THE LEADER IS BEING TELEPORTED TO THE BASE OF OPERATIONS, NEW FREEHOLD. RAVAGE IS OPERATING THE TELEPORTER AND REMAINS BEHIND TO DEAL WITH THE HULK.

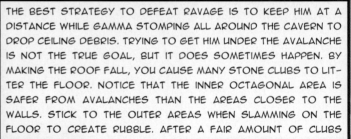

The Leader

THE BEST STRATEGY TO DEFEAT RAVAGE IS TO KEEP HIM AT A DISTANCE WHILE GAMMA STOMPING ALL AROUND THE CAVERN TO DROP CEILING DEBRIS. TRYING TO GET HIM UNDER THE AVALANCHE IS NOT THE TRUE GOAL, BUT IT DOES SOMETIMES HAPPEN. BY MAKING THE ROOF FALL, YOU CAUSE MANY STONE CLUBS TO LITTER THE FLOOR. NOTICE THAT THE INNER OCTAGONAL AREA IS SAFER FROM AVALANCHES THAN THE AREAS CLOSER TO THE WALLS. STICK TO THE OUTER AREAS WHEN SLAMMING ON THE FLOOR TO CREATE RUBBLE. AFTER A FAIR AMOUNT OF CLUBS LITTER THE FLOOR, BEGIN PICKING UP THE CLUBS AND THROWING THEM AT RAVAGE. THIS DOES JUST AS MUCH DAMAGE AS SWINGING THEM AT HIM AND IT'S SAFER DUE TO THE DISTANCE FROM HIM.

Ravage is a tactical fighter, don't leave yourself open.

RAVAGE

IF YOU WISH TO GET YOUR FISTS ON RAVAGE, TRY THIS: TARGET RAVAGE AND PERFORM A CHARGED GAMMA CRUSHER. AFTER YOU POUND THE BOSS, THE GROUND AROUND HIM SHAKES AND CAUSES THE ROOF TO FALL AS HE RECOVERS FROM YOUR HIT. SINCE HE CANNOT MOVE OUT OF THE WAY IN TIME, THE CRUMBLING ROOF FALLS ON HIS HEAD CAUSING MORE DAMAGE! JUST MAKE SURE TO JUMP, OR RUN AWAY AS SOON AS YOU LAND THE ATTACK.

CONTINUE TO RUN AROUND THE OUTER PERIMETER PICKING UP CLUBS AND THROWING THEM AT RAVAGE UNTIL HIS HEALTH IS COMPLETELY DEPLETED. AT THIS POINT, STAGE TWO BEGINS. IN STAGE TWO, RAVAGE RECOVERS HIS HEALTH AND TWO GAMMA ELITE TELEPORT INTO THE CAVERN. HEALTH POWER-UPS ARE AVAILABLE ONLY FROM DEFEATING GAMMA ELITE, SO TAKING THEM OUT MAY BE A NECESSITY.

GAMMA ELITE CONTINUE TO TELEPORT INTO BATTLE AS THE PREVIOUS TWO ARE DEFEATED. CONCENTRATE ATTACKS ON RAVAGE AS MUCH AS POSSIBLE WHEN TAKING ON THE GAMMA ELITE, USE A GRAPPLE MULTI-STRIKE THROW AND AIM FOR THE OTHER GUARD OR RAVAGE. CONTINUE WITH THE CLUB-THROWING STRATEGY AND AVOID CHARGED GAMMA CRUSHERS WHEN THE ARMED ELITE GUARDS ARE AROUND.

ONCE RAVAGE IS BURIED UNDER AN AVALANCHE, BRUCE TELEPORTS TO NEW FREEHOLD IN ATTEMPTS TO FIND LEADER AND GET THE GAMMA ORB BACK.

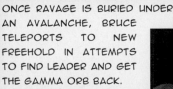

The Leader now has The Gamma Orb and wields the awesome power it contains. The Orb must be destroyed before the Leader can manipulate its power to his own ends.

CELLULAR DISRUPTION

Bruce travels to the New Freehold via teleportation, which happens to disrupt his cellular makeup. It will be a while until the Hulk can make another appearance.

Start on the teleportation pad (**A**) that sits before a large security door on the next platform. Cross the small bridge and walk up to the power obelisks on either side of the door (**B**). Pull the switches on both obelisks to open the large door.

Enter the cave and walk just as far as the second framed archway (**C**). Two Gamma Elite run out from farther down the tunnel. Turn around and run back out of the tunnel and hide behind one of the obelisks.

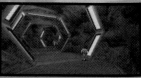

Wait behind the obelisk until both Gamma Elite have exited the tunnel. Sneak around the backside of the obelisk and run into the tunnel. Don't stop running until reaching the next door (**D**) and a cutscene begins. The affects of the teleporter wear off and the Hulk makes an appearance. The battle ahead is against two ex-bosses.

MADMAN & HALF-LIFE

YOU KNOW THE CAPABILITIES OF BOTH MADMAN AND HALF-LIFE. YOU FOUGHT THEM BEFORE, BUT NOW YOU GO UP AGAINST BOTH AT THE SAME TIME. THE GOOD NEWS IS THAT YOU NEED ONLY DEPLETE HALF OF ONE OF THEIR LIFE METERS BEFORE MADMAN ESCAPES THE BATTLE THROUGH ONE OF THE ELEVATORS.

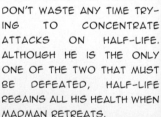

AVOID THE FALLING DEBRIS AND USE THE LARGE BOULDERS AND CLUB-SHAPED STONES AS WEAPONS. USE THE BROKEN OBELISKS AS A DURABLE WEAPON. AVOID RUNNING INTO THE LARGE DOORS AS THEY ARE ELECTRIFIED. REMEMBER THAT TOUCHING HALF-LIFE IS A BAD IDEA, SO USE OBJECTS TO SQUISH HIM OR THROW AT HIM. ALTERNATELY, USE AREA ATTACKS, WHICH IS THE BEST STRATEGY TO USE WHILE FIGHTING THESE TWO.

USING JUMPING CHARGED GAMMA STOMPS ONE AFTER THE OTHER CREATES FALLING DEBRIS THAT CAN DAMAGE THE OPPONENTS. PULL OFF ONE STOMP, THEN JUMP OUT OF THE WAY AND PERFORM ANOTHER. KEEP THIS UP WHILE TRYING TO GET AS CLOSE TO THE BOSSES AS POSSIBLE.

DON'T WASTE ANY TIME TRYING TO CONCENTRATE ATTACKS ON HALF-LIFE. ALTHOUGH HE IS THE ONLY ONE OF THE TWO THAT MUST BE DEFEATED, HALF-LIFE REGAINS ALL HIS HEALTH WHEN MADMAN RETREATS.

Look out for fal

THE JUMPING CHARGED GAMMA STOMP WORKS WELL FOR ANOTHER REASON: NEITHER OF THE BOSSES HAVE THE ABILITY TO COUNTER AIR ATTACKS. REMAIN IN THE AIR FOR A FULL CHARGE AND NEITHER MADMAN NOR HALF-LIFE CAN DO A THING ABOUT IT. JUST DON'T PULL OFF TWO CONSECUTIVE STOMPS IN THE SAME AREA OR THE FALLING DEBRIS MAY HIT THE HULK. ANOTHER SMART MOVE IS TO PICK UP MADMAN AND THROW HIM INTO THE ELECTRICALLY CHARGED HALF-LIFE!

MADMAN & HALF-LIFE

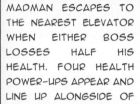

MADMAN ESCAPES TO THE NEAREST ELEVATOR WHEN EITHER BOSS LOSES HALF HIS HEALTH. FOUR HEALTH POWER-UPS APPEAR AND LINE UP ALONGSIDE OF THE SAME ELEVATOR. THESE SHOULD BE MORE THAN ENOUGH TO FULLY REPLENISH THE HULK'S HEALTH AND PREPARE YOU FOR WHAT REMAINS OF THE BATTLE.

YOU COULD CONTINUE TO EXECUTE GAMMA STOMPS, BUT THAT MAY TAKE A WHILE. THERE IS MORE TIME TO MANEUVER AROUND THE BATTLEFIELD WITH MADMAN GONE, SO TAKE FULL ADVANTAGE. CONTINUE TO STOMP WHENEVER YOU NEED AN OBJECT TO USE AGAINST HALF-LIFE. USE THE CLUBS AND OBELISK FRAGMENTS AS WEAPONS AGAINST HALF-LIFE. LURE HIM IN FRONT OF ONE OF THE ELECTRIFIED DOORS AND THROW AN OBJECT TO TRY TO KNOCK HIM INTO THE DOOR. IT DOES NICE DAMAGES, BUT NOT AS WELL AS THE GENERATORS FROM THE FIRST BATTLE.

AFTER DEFEATING HALF-LIFE, PICK UP ANY REMAINING HEALTH POWER-UPS BY THE ELEVATOR OR THE ONE THAT APPEARS ON HIS BODY AFTER HE'S DEFEATED.

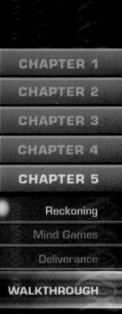
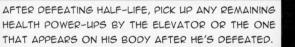

DESTROY THE OBELISKS

After defeating the bosses, the next objective is to destroy the Obelisks, which opens the door [**I**] that leads to the Leader's lair. There are nineteen Obelisks in all, although some may have been taken out already. Confirm that the Obelisks in the boss battle area [**E**] have been destroyed, then bash down the door used to entered the area [**D**] and head back to the teleporter room [**B**] where the level began. Destroy the Obelisks there, then return to the boss battle area [**E**]. Of course, Leader would-n't let you get away with all this without a fight. In the teleporter room, two Gamma Elites appear and attack. Since this happens every step of the way, it's best to destroy enemies as you encounter them, otherwise they start ganging up in larger and larger groups.

The quickest way to destroy Obelisks is by throwing an object at them. The next best thing is to beat them with pieces of another Obelisk. The quicker they are destroyed, the quicker you can get on with defeating the guards and the next set of Obelisks.

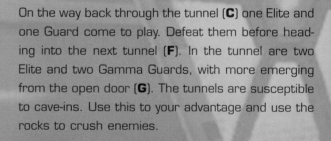

On the way back through the tunnel [**C**] one Elite and one Guard come to play. Defeat them before heading into the next tunnel [**F**]. In the tunnel are two Elite and two Gamma Guards, with more emerging from the open door [**G**]. The tunnels are susceptible to cave-ins. Use this to your advantage and use the rocks to crush enemies.

Take out the autogun on ledge [**G**], then destroy the two Obelisks using the barrel from the autogun. Of course, you could throw enemies into the Obelisks, killing two birds with one stone.

CLOVERLEAF CAVERN

In the large cavern shaped like a cloverleaf are three unopened doors and nine Obelisks (including the two you may have destroyed on the previous ledge). Begin by destroying the largest Obelisks that sits in the middle of the cave, then move forward to the ledge with the auto-gun and take out that piece of artillery on the blue door ledge. Head around to the remaining ledges and destroy all the Obelisks in the cave. Doing so unlocks doors (**H**) and (**J**).

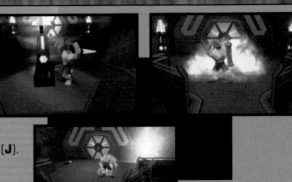

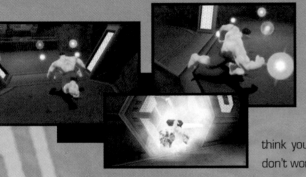

Access ledge (**L**) through door (**J**). The ledge has the power-ups on it that were visible from the boss battle arena (**E**). Visiting it is optional as there are no Obelisks to destroy. If health is needed before the battle waiting on the other side of the Yellow Door, then tear through the Green Door now. If you think you can make it through the tunnel without more Health, then don't worry about heading through the Green Door for the ledge (**L**). On this ledge are three minor and two major Health and a major Rage power-up.

YELLOW DOOR

Tear down the Yellow Door (**H**). In the tunnel beyond the Yellow Door are two Gamma Elite and two Gamma Guards. Defeat them and head to the following cave (**K**). In the cave are four Obelisks, two elevators and a bunch of Health and Rage power-ups. When the elevators arrive, Gamma Elite and Gamma Guards pour out. Destroy the Obelisks quickly in between punches and get back to tunnel. The Guards keep coming as long as you remain in this area. Destroying the last Obelisk unlocks the Blue Door (**I**), which is the final tunnel that leads to the Leader.

Bust through the Yellow Door and run around the huge boulders in the tunnel entrance. Use the large rocks to crush any pursuers and to defeat Guards advancing in the direction you're headed.

BLUE DOOR

There are no enemies to defeat in the tunnel beyond the Blue Door and the Blue Door (**I**) itself has opened. If you are alive, there's no reason to head through the Green Door (**J**) to get health. Just run through the tunnel and near the end as you approach another door (**M**). Time to battle The Leader.

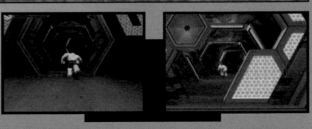

119

MIND GAMES

You've come this far and now it's time to face The Leader himself.

THE LEADER IS A DEVIOUS AND MANIPULATIVE MUTANT. BENT ON CONTROLLING EVERYTHING AROUND HIM, HE HOPES TO HARNESS THE POWER OF THE HULK FOR HIS OWN ENDS. POWER-HUNGRY AND CRUEL, THE LEADER STOPS AT NOTHING IN HIS QUEST TO REALIZE HIS VISION OF A DOMINANT GAMMA-POWERED RACE. THE LEADER CONTROLS HIS ELITE FORCES: THE ALPHA GUARD AND THE GAMMA GUARD. HALF-LIFE, MADMAN AND CRAWFORD (AKA RAVAGE) ALL REPORT TO HIM. THE LEADER AND MADMAN ARE BIOLOGICAL BROTHERS.

THE LEADER

BOSS ATTRIBUTES

THE LEADER IS ONE TOUGH COOKIE WITH MANY TRICKS UP HIS PURPLE SLEEVE. HE USES MIND BEAMS AS EASILY AS OTHER PEOPLE BLINK THEIR EYES. THESE ARE ANY SINGLE BEAM BLAST USED BY THE LEADER, RECOGNIZABLE BY THEIR ORANGE GLOW AND LONG RANGE ABILITIES.

LEADER USES HIS BIG OL' HEAD AND SWOLLEN BRAIN TO PERFORM TELEKINESIS. THIS GIVES HIM THE ABILITY TO STUN THE HULK, THEN QUICKLY FOLLOW IT UP WITH A TELEKINETIC TOSS.

WHEN THE LEADER WARMS UP TO USE A SUPER MIND BEAM, WATCH OUT! THE LEADER TELEPORTS TO A SPOT AND ROTATES, BLASTING THE ENTIRE CHAMBER WITH A LONG ORANGE LASER BEAM. WHILE HE SETTING UP AND PERFORMING THIS ATTACK, HE IS UNTOUCHABLE. THE BEST WAY TO AVOID THIS ATTACK IS TO JUMP INTO THE AIR JUST BEFORE THE LASER REACHES YOU, THEN CHARGE A JUMP ATTACK TO REMAIN SUSPENDED IN THE AIR.

THE BATTLE ENVIRONMENT

THE BATTLE ARENA IS A FAIRLY LARGE ONE AND CONSISTS OF FOUR OBELISKS THAT CAN BE USED AS WEAPONS. THERE ARE TWO ELEVATORS THAT DELIVER TEAMS OF TWO GAMMA ELITE GUARDS. THE ELEVATORS' EXTERIORS CAN BE USED TO TEMPORARILY HIDE FROM DANGER. THE ONLY HEALTH POWER-UPS AVAILABLE APPEAR FROM DEFEATING GAMMA ELITE AND THE LEADER'S TELEKINETIC CLONES.

THE PRE-BATTLE

BEFORE THE BATTLE WITH LEADER BEGINS, DIRECT BRUCE BANNER TO PULL THE LEVERS OF FOUR OBELISKS TO POWER DOWN THE FORCE FIELD AROUND THE GAMMA ORB IN THE BACK OF THE ROOM. ALL THE WHILE, THE LEADER IS BREATHING DOWN YOUR NECK AND OCCASIONALLY STRIKING WITH A TELEKINETIC BLAST. HIDE BEHIND THE OBELISKS TO AVOID THE ATTACK, BUT THERE'S NO NEED. YOU SHOULD HAVE ENOUGH HEALTH TO RUN UP TO EACH OBELISK, PULL THE LEVERS, THEN RUN TO THE GAMMA ORB EVEN IF THE LEADER ZAPS YOU THREE TIMES (THE NUMBER OF TIMES HE HITS IF YOU RUN FROM ONE TO THE OTHER WITHOUT PAUSING).

ONCE YOU TAKE THE ORB BACK, AND BRUCE HAS THE ABILITY TO TRANS-FORM BACK INTO THE HULK. THE HULK VS. THE LEADER BATTLE BEGINS.

SMASH

FAKE OUT

BEST TACTIC: THE FAKE. RUN FOR ONE OBELISK, WAIT UNTIL LEADER TELE-PORTS IN, THEN DASH FOR ANOTHER OBELISK. EVEN IF THE LEADER ATTACKS, YOU'LL HAVE ESCAPED HIS RANGE AND HAVE PLENTY OF TIME TO PULL THE LEVER BEFORE HE CAN FOLLOW UP AND ATTACK.

THE HULK VS. THE LEADER THE GAMMA CRUSHER

THE KEY TO BEATING LEADER IS THE EFFECTIVE USE OF MULTIPLE CHARGED JUMPING ATTACKS, NAMELY THE GAMMA CRUSHER. BE SURE TO TARGET THE ENEMY YOU WANT TO HIT, AND THAT TARGET IS WITH-IN THE ATTACK'S RANGE. IF YOU FALL SHORT OF YOUR TARGET, YOU ARE LEFT WIDE OPEN FOR ATTACKS.

BEGIN THE BATTLE RUNNING UP TO THE LEADER, JUMP INTO THE AIR, AND FULLY CHARGE A GAMMA CRUSHER. THIS TAKES 1/10 OF HIS HEALTH. YES, IT'S GOING TO BE A LONG AND TOUGH BATTLE. THE BENEFIT TO THE JUMPING ATTACK IS THAT IT AVOIDS THE LEADER'S BEAM ATTACK AND CHARGES YOUR ATTACK AT THE SAME TIME. AS BIG AS THE LEADER'S BRAIN IS, HE CAN'T FIGURE OUT HOW TO AIM HIS ATTACK UPWARD!

AVOIDING THE SUPER MIND BEAM

WHEN THE BOSS TELEPORTS TO THE BACK OF THE ROOM, HE IS MOST LIKELY (BUT NOT ALWAYS) PREPARING USE A SUPER MIND BEAM. DO NOT ATTACK HIM WHEN HE BEGINS *OR* WHILE HE IS PERFORMING THE ATTACK; HE IS INVULNERA-BLE. JUMP OVER THE LARGE BEAM OR SUFFER A BAD CRASH AND BURN. SUPER MIND BEAM HAS A LONG RECOVERY TIME, LEAVING THE LEADER OPEN FOR A COMBO OR OTHER BIG ATTACK. MOST OF THE TIME, THIS MOVE IS PERFORMED WHEN THE LEADER IS NEAR THE GAMMA ORB, BUT SOMETIMES HE PERFORMS THIS IN THE MIDDLE OF THE ARENA. WHENEVER YOU SEE THE LEADER TELEPORT (HE DISAPPEARS IN A BEAM OF BRIGHT WHITE LIGHT), BE READY.

NEUTRALIZE THE MIND BEAM BOW

WATCH THE LEADER'S EVERY MOVE CLOSELY. LEARN TO RECOGNIZE WHAT HE DOES JUST BEFORE EACH ATTACK AND HALF OF THE BATTLE IS WON. WHEN HE THROWS HIS ARMS BACK AND BEGINS TO GLOW, HIS NEXT MOVE INCLUDES FRAYED LASER BEAMS RAINING DOWN IN THE IMMEDIATE AREA IN FRONT OF HIM. IF YOU ARE IN THE AIR AND READY TO UNLEASH ANOTHER GAMMA CRUSHER ON HIM, GO AHEAD AND RELEASE THE ATTACK BEFORE HE RELEASES HIS. YOU WON'T DAMAGE HIM WHILE HE IS SETTING UP THE ATTACK BUT YOU LAND BEHIND HIM, AND ARE SAFE (90% OF THE TIME) FROM THIS ATTACK. WHILE BEHIND HIM, TAKE THE OPPORTUNITY TO ATTACK DURING THE RECOVERY FROM HIS EXHAUSTING ATTACK.

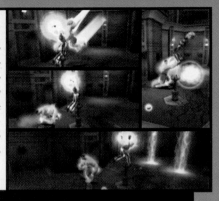

CLOWNING WITH THE TELEKINETIC CLONES

WHEN THE LEADER CREATES THREE CLONES OF HIMSELF IT'S OBVIOUS. A CUTSCENE SHOWS THEM LINING UP ALONG THE ENTRANCE. DON'T WORRY ABOUT TRYING TO FIND THE LEADER OUT OF THIS CLUSTER, JUST RUN, JUMP, AND GAMMA CRUSH AS MANY OF THEM AS POSSIBLE. HALF OF THE TIME THESE CLONES PRODUCE A HEALTH POWER-UP. ONE GOOD HIT OR A FEW WEAK ONES SHOULD ELIMINATE A CLONE. LOOK UP AT THE HEALTH METER WHILE HITTING A LEADER TO SEE IF THE METER QUICKLY DEPLETES (IT'S A CLONE), OR DOESN'T (THE REAL LEADER). ALSO, CLONES ONLY KNOW ONE ATTACK, THE MIND BEAM LASER.

STAGE TWO

WHEN HIS HEALTH IS GONE THE FIRST TIME, THE LEADER SHRUGS AND LAUGHS IT OFF AS HIS HEALTH METER FULLY REPLENISHES. AT THIS TIME, THE TWO ELEVATORS DELIVER ONE GAMMA ELITE APIECE. WHEN THE GAMMA ELITE SHOW UP, THEY ARE THE MAIN PRIORITY. THEIR LASER GUNS CAN REALLY SUBTRACT HEALTH QUICKLY. USE JUMPING ATTACKS, BUT BE QUICK ABOUT THEM AND DON'T EVEN THINK ABOUT CHARGING THE ATTACK, OR THEIR GUNS PICK YOU OUT OF THE AIR. IF THE ODDS GROW BEYOND WHAT YOU CAN REASONABLY HANDLE, RUN AROUND THE SIDE OF AN ELEVATOR AND WAIT UNTIL THEY COME TO YOU. WHEN THEY NEAR, SLIP AROUND THE CORNER AND PERFORM A MULTI-STRIKE THROW GRAPPLE ATTACK. PICK UP ANY HEALTH POWER-UPS THAT APPEAR.

ELEVATOR CHEAT

IT'S POSSIBLE TO RUN UP TO EITHER ONE OF THE ELEVATORS BEFORE THE DOORS OPEN AND BEGIN BEATING ON THE GAMMA ELITE AS SOON AS THE DOORS OPEN. KEEP THE PRESSURE ON THEM UNTIL THE DOOR CLOSES, TRAPPING THE ELITE IN THE ELEVATOR! WHEN THIS HAPPENS, AND YOU DEFEAT THE REMAINING GUARD, THE GAME DOESN'T REGISTER THE DEFEAT OF BOTH GUARDS AND DOESN'T SEND MORE GUARDS DOWN INTO THE BATTLE. THIS DOES HAVE A DRAWBACK IN THAT GAMMA ELITE PRODUCE HEALTH POWER-UPS AFTER YOU DEFEAT THEM. THIS LEAVES JUST YOU AND THE LEADER TO BATTLE ALONE.

FOLLOWING THE LEADER...

WHEN YOU COMPLETELY REMOVE THE LEADER'S SECOND HEALTH METER, YOU WIN THE BATTLE. THE LEADER TELEPORTS TO WHO KNOWS WHERE AS THE CAVE BEGINS CRUMBLE. YOU MUST ESCAPE THE CAVE BEFORE BEING BURIED IN A PILE OF RUBBLE.

THE LEADER

Freehold is collapsing, get out! There are multiple routes available but only one is the way out. The Leader's army will do anything to bury the Hulk alive.

ESCAPING FREEHOLD

The Leader has escaped, and the entire base is collapsing on itself. If you don't want to be buried with it, you need to get moving! Run out of Leader's lair and into the tunnel heading for the cloverleaf-shaped cave. You run across some Gamma Elite along the way, but don't worry about them. They're trying to escape with their lives as well.

CRUSH

TIME LIMIT?

THERE IS NO NEED TO GET NERVOUS ABOUT ESCAPING THE BASE BEFORE THE WHOLE COMPLEX CAVES-IN ON YOU. THERE IS NO TIME LIMIT AND NO MASSIVE CAVE-IN IS GOING TO OCCUR. THE ONLY THING TO WATCH OUT FOR IS THE INCREASED OCCURRENCES OF FALLING ROCKS. TO STAY SAFE, LOOK FOR THE EARLY WARNING OF WATER AND DUST THAT FALLS JUST BEFORE THE ROCKS COME DOWN. YOU CAN ACTUALLY EXPLORE THE OTHER TUNNELS AND LEDGES WITHOUT A CONCERN FOR TIME. HOWEVER, THERE ARE NO POWER-UPS OR ANYTHING SPECIAL ON THE OTHER PATHWAYS, EXCEPT FOR MORE FLEEING GAMMA ELITE.

From the cloverleaf cave, continue running forward through the broken white door (**B**) and the following tunnel. If the Gamma Elite are running ahead of you, they will stop before crossing the bridge in the following cave (**C**). They must sense danger and know the bridge is going to collapse.

The bridge collapses in two pieces. The first section (**C**) collapses before the second piece (**D**). The collapse doesn't begin to collapse until you cross the first section. Jump to the second section as the collapse is occurring, then jump again as the second section begins to crumble. Continue through the following tunnel and the door automatically opens. In the teleporter room is Madman, waiting for you, not worried in the slightest bit that the base is falling in on itself.

MADMAN

MADMAN RAN AWAY FROM THE LAST FIGHT, BUT THIS TIME HE'S GOING TO STICK AROUND TO TRY TO FINISH THE JOB. MADMAN USES HIS GROUND STOMPING ATTACK LIKE THERE IS NO TOMORROW (WELL, FOR HIM, THERE ISN'T GOING TO BE A TOMORROW).

SPEED UP THE COLLAPSE OF THE CEILING BY POUNDING ON THE GROUND. SINCE MADMAN FOLLOWS YOU EVERYWHERE YOU GO, POUND ON THE GROUND AND MOVE AWAY TO LURE MADMAN INTO THE FALLING ROCKS.

USE THE LARGE STONE CLUBS AS PROJECTILES AND WHEN MADMAN IS NOT ENGAGED IN HIS GROUND STOMPING MOVE, USE GAMMA CRUSHER ON HIM. USING GAMMA CRUSHER DURING HIS GROUND STOMPING IS USELESS AS HE'S INVULNERABLE DURING HIS ATTACK. IF YOU BECOME ENRAGED, FOUR GAMMA CRUSHERS TAKE AWAY HALF HIS HEALTH. ALL IN ALL, IT'S NOT A TOUGH FIGHT AND GOOD, LENGTHY COMBOS SHOULD DO HIM IN QUICKLY.

MADMAN

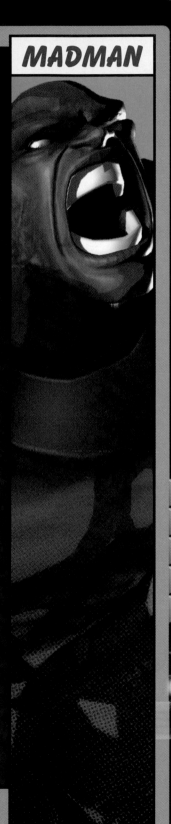

CHAPTER 1

CHAPTER 2

CHAPTER 3

CHAPTER 4

CHAPTER 5

Reckoning

Mind Games

Deliverance

WALKTHROUGH

CHALLENGE MODE

There are five games in Challenge Mode, all of which are locked at the beginning of the game. To unlock the Challenge Mode games you must complete certain levels in Story Mode.

CHALLENGE MODE UNLOCKING TABLE

CHALLENGE GAME	BEAT STORY MODE LEVEL	LEVEL BOSS
ENDURANCE MODE 1	LVL 6: A DIFFERENT BREED	HALF-LIFE
ENDURANCE MODE 3	LVL 18: ONE AND ALL	RAVAGE
TIME ATTACK MODE 1	LVL 10: SAVIOR	MADMAN
TIME ATTACK MODE 2	LVL 21: DELIVERANCE	MADMAN
HULK SMASH! MODE	LVL 14: GUARDIAN	FLUX

Completing Challenge Mode games unlocks nothing but gives you bragging rights when you beat the high score.

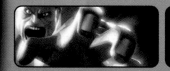

ENDURANCE MODE 1

In Endurance Mode 1 there is no time limit. You fight as long as you can survive the "Waves" of attacks. One point is earned for each kill. If you use combos to eliminate an enemy, then you get a point for each hit landed on that enemy, tallied after you take him out. Each "Wave" brings different types or amounts of enemies and the objects in the environment may change.

For example, in Wave 1 of Endurance Mode 1 there is a forklift, a large shipping container, pipes, girders and barrels. The enemies are Rifle Soldiers only. During Wave 2, all the floor items remain the same, but soldiers appear on some scaffolding against the walls. In Wave 3, Rocket Soldiers are added to the mix along with some newly placed parking curbs. During Wave 5, the floor items change dramatically as large gas tanks are lined up in a circle in the middle of the floor. The enemies include Gamma Dogs. Cars enter the room in Wave 6 and beyond that it's just a combination of everything. In Wave 15 (if you live that long to see it) you begin in the middle of the room surrounded by cars and storage containers. In Wave 20 you're surrounded by Shock Troopers, but Wave 21 is the best, you become surrounded by a bunch of Major Health power-ups! You continue to see more Missile Soldiers, Shockshielders, Gamma Dogs, and plenty of Rifle Soldiers.

SMASH

SURVIVAL TIP

DEFEAT ENEMIES IN THIS ORDER WHEN PRESENT: GAMMA DOGS, MISSILE SOLDIERS, SHOCKSHIELDERS, RIFLE SOLDIERS.

MISSILE SOLDIERS LIKE TO HIDE IN THE FOUR CORNERS OF THE ROOM. RUN AND JUMP WHEN YOU HEAR A ROCKET BEING LAUNCHED. THROW GIRDERS OR PIPES AT THE MISSILE SOLDIERS TO SAVE YOU THE TRIP. COLLECT HEALTH POWER-UPS AS QUICKLY AS POSSIBLE AND DON'T SHY AWAY FROM THE RAGE POWER-UPS. WHENEVER THE HULK BECOMES ENRAGED, RUN TO THE MIDDLE OF THE ACTION AND USE A SUPER OVERHAND SMASH TO ANNIHILATE EVERYTHING IN SIGHT. IDEALLY, USE WHAT YOU CAN WHILE ENRAGED AND JUST BEFORE THE RAGE IS DEPLETED, PULL OFF THE SUPER OVERHAND SMASH!

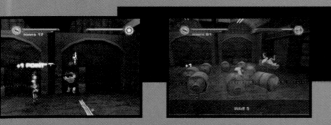

ENDURANCE MODE 2

Endurance Mode 2 takes place in the Alcatraz mystery hangar. Enemies include Gamma Guards, Alpha Soldiers, Gamma Dogs, Alpha Missiles, and Alpha Shielders. In Wave 5, autoguns pop up in the center of the room and around the perimeter! Take these out with explosive barrels or heavy objects before they slowly eat away your health. Objects found around the hangar include barrels, shipping containers, crates scrap metal, gas tanks, rusty pipes, and forklifts.

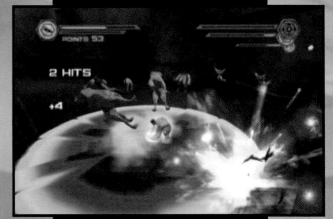

CRUSH

SURVIVING WAVE 5

THE KEY TO SURVIVING THE AUTOGUNS IS TO STAY AWAY
FROM THE CENTER OF THE HANGAR WHERE ALL THE GUNS CAN
SHOOT AT YOU AT ONCE. THEY POP OUT AND SHOOT WHEN
YOU'RE NEAR THEM. GAMMA DOGS, GAMMA GUARDS, AND
ALPHA MISSILES PUMMEL YOU WHILE YOU ARE TRYING TO
TAKE OUT THE CANNONS. DESTROY THEM AND PICK UP ALL
THE RAGE POWER-UPS. WHEN YOU ENTER RAGE MODE, RUN
(ALLOW THE ENEMY TO FOLLOW YOU) TO AN AUTOGUN AND
LET LOOSE THE SUPER OVERHAND SMASH WHEN THE ENEMIES
ARE GATHERED AROUND THE AUTOGUN. REPEAT THIS
PROCESS AS LONG AS THE AREA IS CROWDED WITH ENEMIES.
WHEN IT CLEARS OUT A BIT, GRAB PROJECTILES AND JUMP
AND THROW THE SCRAP AT THE REMAINING AUTOGUNS.

WAVE 5

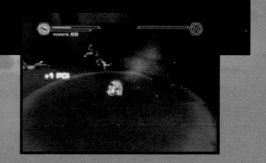

Endurance
Mode 1

**Endurance
Mode 2**

Time Attack
Mode 1

Time Attack
Mode 2

Hulk Smash! Mode

CHALLENGE MODE

TIME ATTACK MODE 1

In Time Attack Mode 1 you must survive the waves of attacking soldiers for four minutes. The point system is the same as in Endurance Mode. You face Soldiers, Shock Troopers, Rifle Soldiers, and Shockshielders. This is a fun challenge, especially when you start throwing soldier after solder over the edge of the building. There are plenty of major Health power-ups to be found when defeating the soldiers and survival is never really an issue. Use Super Overhand Smash to clear the area when you enter Rage Mode. There are plenty of barrels, condenser units, rocks, forklifts and pipe to keep the action going. Try to hit the helicopters that circle the building as Wave 5 begins.

Endurance
Mode 1

Endurance
Mode 2

Time Attack
Mode 1

Time Attack
Mode 2

Hulk Smash! Mode

CHALLENGE MODE

Helicopters are vulnerable to projectiles.

When you have only 20 seconds remaining in the challenge, a cutscene faces you to the center glass room and in front of a regenerating barrel. Grab barrel after barrel and throw them at the lineup of Shockshielders at the opposite end of the room.

TIME ATTACK MODE 2

Time Attack Mode 2 takes place in a Robot lab inside the Desert Base (Spearpoint level). Like the first Time Attack challenge, you have four minutes to survive Waves of enemy attacks. The points scored are tallied as they are in previous modes. You fight Shock Troopers, Rifle Soldiers, Missile Soldiers, Gamma Dogs, Robots, and Shockshielders. The objects found in the room include, spool-shaped tables, large generator pipes, gas tanks, explosive barrels, parking curbs, and shipping containers.

The Robot enters the fight in Wave 6, so be prepared. You have access to two labs, so make use of the space and the array of objects. Try leading the enemy through the hallway that connects the two rooms. Grab a large object, like a shipping container, and smash them like ants as they file into the room.

Endurance
Mode 1

Endurance
Mode 2

Time Attack
Mode 1

Time Attack
Mode 2

Hulk Smash! Mode

CHALLENGE MODE

HULK SMASH

Hulk Smash is very similar to Time Attack mode in that you have four minutes to survive the challenge and the enemy kill point system is the same. The difference with Hulk Smash is that there are more objects around to smash and you get a point for each object destroyed. The environment will seem familiar. It's the first train depot from level 5 "End of the Line." The enemies encountered include Shock Troopers, Rifle Soldiers, Missile Soldiers, Gamma Dogs, and Shockshielders. Outside are such objects as train cars, towers, a forklift, and a storage container. Inside are train cars, storage containers, generator fence poles, a forklift, three cars, barrels, and a gas tank. Just smash everything and grab the big stuff to crush the puny humans.

Endurance Mode 1

Endurance Mode 2

Time Attack Mode 1

Time Attack Mode 2

Hulk Smash! Mode

CHALLENGE MODE

There are two types of codes in Hulk: the traditional Cheat Codes and special Universal Unlock Codes, which unlock bonus materials.

CHEAT CODES

From the Main Menu, enter "Options," then "Code Input." On the Code Input screen there are 7 spaces to enter a code. Do not press "Accept" until you have entered the entire string or you must start over.

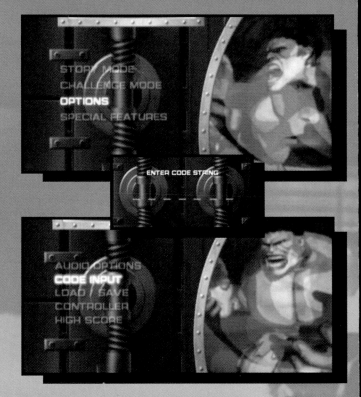

Once you have entered a valid code, go back to the Main Menu, select "Special Features" and "Cheats." The Cheats menu tells you what cheats have been unlocked. Select the Cheat you wish to activate or deactivate.

For the "unlock all levels" cheat, you may then go back to the Main Menu, choose "Story Mode", then "Continue Game" and browse all of the levels to select and play any level in the game.

CHEAT CODES

DESCRIPTION	CODE INPUT
INVULNERABILITY	GMMSKIN
REGENERATOR	FLSHWND
UNLIMITED CONTINUES	GRNCHTR
DOUBLE HULK HP	HLTHOSE
DOUBLE ENEMIES HP	BRNGITN
HALF ENEMIES HP	MMMYHLP
RESET HIGH SCORE	NMBTHIH
UNLOCK ALL LEVELS	TRUBLVR

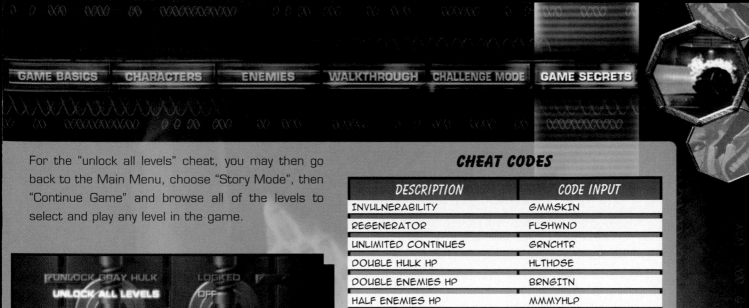

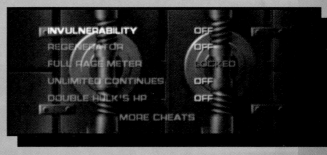

UNLOCKING CHALLENGE MODE GAMES

CHALLENGE MODE UNLOCKING TABLE

CHALLENGE GAME	BEAT STORY MODE LEVEL	LEVEL BOSS
ENDURANCE MODE 1	LVL 6: A DIFFERENT BREED	HALF-LIFE
ENDURANCE MODE 3	LVL 18: ONE AND ALL	RAVAGE
TIME ATTACK MODE 1	LVL 10: SAVIOR	MADMAN
TIME ATTACK MODE 2	LVL 21: DELIVERANCE	MADMAN
HULK SMASH! MODE	LVL 14: GUARDIAN	FLUX

CONTINUE GAME

After completing all the levels in Story Mode, return to the Story Mode menu and the "Continue Game" option will be available. "Continue Game" allows you to select and play any level from the game. When you turn on the console, you must load your "complete" game save before this option is available.

RADICAL ENTERTAINMENT: OUR STUDIO

Pioneering the future of entertainment is no easy task. Creating entertainment that captures the world's imagination begins with inspiring our own, so we've worked hard to cultivate an environment that both cultivates and rewards creativity.

Please the eye, comfort the body, stir the mind - these were our goals when designing our space. The 50,000 square foot studio boasts a stocked kitchen, indoor log cabin, and every tool our team needs to push the boundaries of interactive entertainment.

Radical's Vancouver, Canada office is one part studio, one part campus, one part playground. And not a single cubicle in sight.

Radical isn't just a cool job in a cool office - it's what we love to do, where we love to do it.

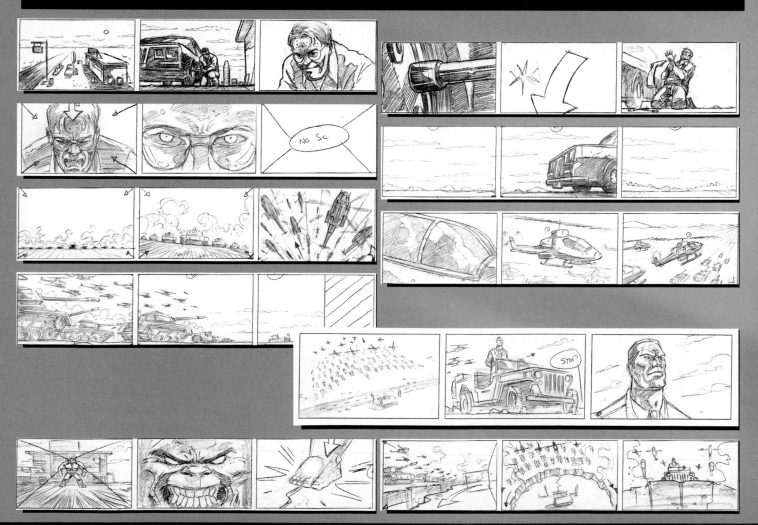

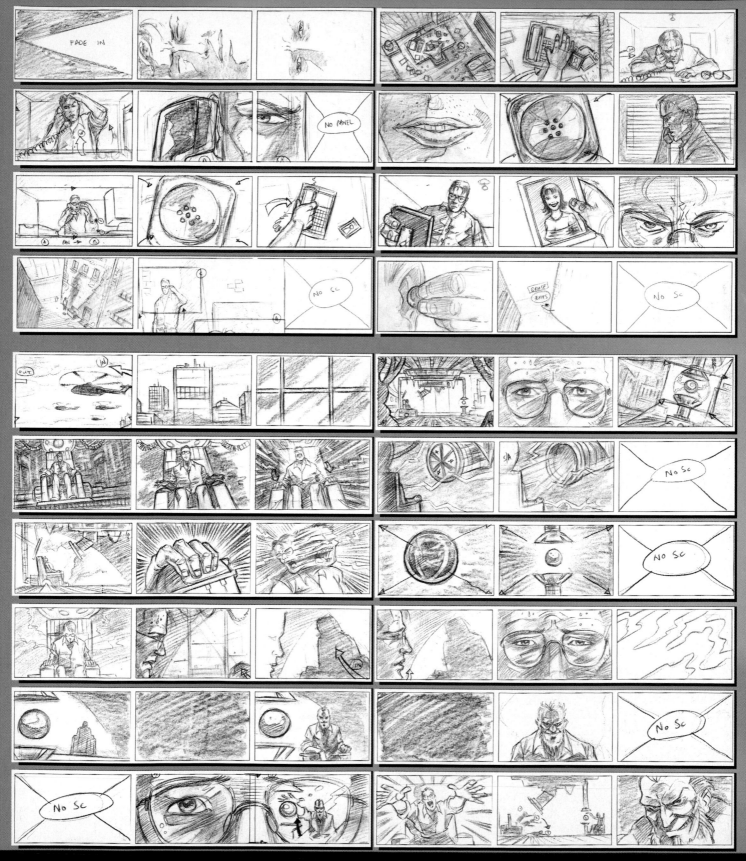

GERALD SOMBILON

3D CHARACTER ANIMATOR

Hobbies
I enjoy playing sports and spending time with my family and friends.

Major Titles Worked On
This is my first major title. I came from a television background where I worked on projects such as Beast Machines, Action Man, Heavy Gear, and Max Steel.

Favorite Food to Snack on While Gaming
BBQ potato chips

Favorite Movie
Too many to pick just one. Fight Club, Unbreakable, Fellowship of The Ring, and Matrix rank pretty high up there. Die Hard is an oldie but a goodie.

Most Recent Gaming Obsession
The Hulk.

What role did you play in the Hulk project? Or, what did your specific day-to-day tasks include?
I was the animator for the pre-rendered cinematics on the Hulk.

Upon discovering that Radical was asked to develop The Hulk, what was your immediate "gut reaction" about being given the opportunity?
Incredible opportunity.

The Hulk is one of the most recognizable comic book licenses. What characteristics did you want to capture in the game?
Hulk's sheer strength and power. Oh yeah, and apparently he likes to smash stuff.

Was motion capture used for this game? If so, what was the process?
Motion capture was used in the cinematics for a good portion of the Banner dialogue scenes. It was important for us to get accurate movements of Banner and Betty and then exploit the key framing aspects with the supernatural characters as the Hulk and the other super villains. Those characters really push the envelope on poses–movements like that would be impossible for any motion capture actor to perform.

What was your favorite aspect about this project?
Definitely the delivery of the final product. It is the moment when you look back at all the adversity, hard work, and endless hours that you and your team put in and you say to yourself: it was all worth it!

After completing the game, what do you expect/want people to say about their gaming experience?
Cinematics allow gamers to take a break from their efforts and just be entertained, so I'm hoping that mixing the dynamic of a story into the dynamic of a game raises the gameplay experience to another level.

What are you most proud of concerning the game?
My team.

There are a lot of industries that require a person with your talents. What is it about the gaming industry that pulled you in and keeps you here?
Basically the opportunity to work with a team of incredibly talented and inspiring individuals.

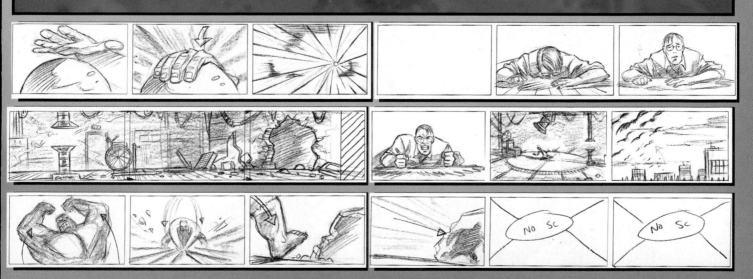

Martin Bae

Hobbies
I play golf every chance I get so I guess that's my only hobby at the moment.

Major Titles Worked On
I've worked on children's interactive titles mostly in the past before moving into film and television production. Have you ever seen a sci-fi flick called "Laserhawk"?

Favorite Food to Snack on While Gaming
Mac n' Cheese.

Favorite Movie
I love foreign films, especially Zhang Yimou films; did I ask if you've seen "Laserhawk"?

Most Recent Gaming Obsession
Soul Calibur 2

What role did you play in the Hulk project? Or, what did your specific day-to-day tasks include?
My daily role on this game was to provide direction to maintain a consistent look and feel for all art content development. I've worked closely with storyboard artists, modelers, animators and special f/x artists to create content that reflects our overall creative vision and what people will come to expect when they play our game.

Upon discovering that Radical was asked to develop The Hulk, what was your immediate "gut reaction" about being given the opportunity?
Awesome! The opportunity to work on a game based on a Marvel character whose comics I grew up reading as a child really got me excited.

When developing the concept art and storyboards, were there any elements that simply had to make the game?
Definitely. We drew some inspiration and vision from the comic book series and just a little from the television series. In fact, one of our cut scenes has our Bruce Banner saying the classic line, "Don't make me angry. You wouldn't like me when I'm angry". Very cool line.

How did you manage to capture the feel of the movie and comics?
The game is definitely an extension of the Hulk movie. Our game storyline takes place a year after the film story so we introduced the same characters and some locations from the film as well as characters that appear in the Hulk comics. Our overall presentation goal was to make the Hulk game experience look and feel like an interactive comic book by integrating a cell-shaded style over highly detailed environments.

What was it about the license that was the hardest to work with? The easiest?
I grew up reading Hulk comics and watching the Hulk television series so I guess the toughest part about working on this game was keeping a fair distance from the Marvel comic universe and not to draw too much inspiration from that and the television series since this game is based on the Hulk film. The easiest part is knowing that whatever version of the Hulk people will be familiar with whether it be comics, television, cartoons or the film, everyone knows that the Hulk is green.

What was your favorite aspect about this project?
My favorite aspect about this project is the overall presentation of the Hulk license. I truly believe we have delivered on the expectations of many who will play this game.

After completing the game, what do you expect/want people to say about their gaming experience?
I want people to say that this game has set a higher benchmark for character-based games and that they've fully experienced what it's like to become the Hulk.

What are you most proud of concerning the game?
Teamwork. I'm proud to have been part of a team that worked like a family.

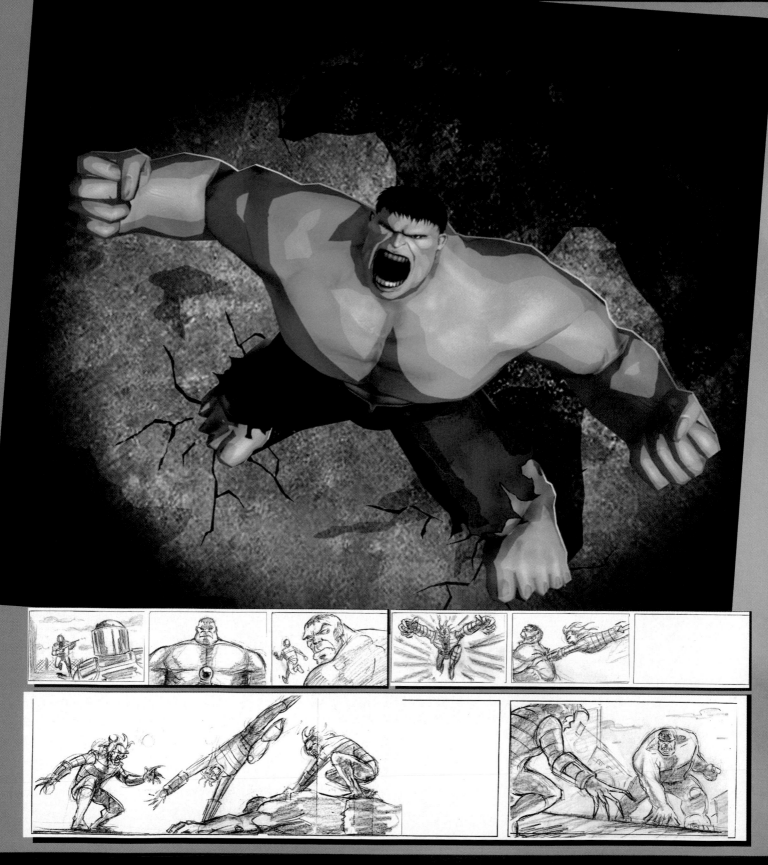

GRAIG ROBERTSON

Hobbies
Playing the Saxophone and writing music for my band
'Mr.Scene', Rock Climbing, Mountain Biking.

Major Titles Worked On
Hulk, Dark Angel, CSI, Simpsons Road Rage, Jackie Chan's
Stuntmaster, Fox Hockey 2000, Power Play '98 Hockey, Sega
All Star Hockey '98.

Favorite Food to Snack on While Gaming
Oatmeal

Favorite Movie
Videodrome

Most Recent Gaming Obsession
Besides Hulk, State of Emergency as stress relief

**What role did you play in the Hulk project? Or, what did
your specific day-to-day tasks include?**
I set the vision for the sound design and the music, Designed
some new in house audio tools for implementing the design,
Composed the music, Deep Heavy Breathing.

**Upon discovering that Radical was asked to develop The
Hulk, what was your immediate "gut reaction" about
being given the opportunity?**
I was stoked. I loved the Hulk comic books as a kid and I
watched the TV show with Bill Bixby.

**What inspirations did you draw for the game (personal
music favorites, etc.)? Was there a "mood" that you
were shooting for?**
I would say that the music was influenced by Stravinsky,
Bernard Herman and world music, i.e.: African, Japanese
Koto drums and even Balinese music for the Gamma dogs.

I tried to Juxtapose Banner music from Hulk music yet slowly
merge elements of Hulk music into the Banner music as the
game story unfolds. Banner music is a moody orchestral
treatment; somewhat disturbed with incursions of other
themes such as military, or 'weird science' synthesis. Hulk
music is a fusion of primal / tribal rhythms and orchestral. At
times, Hulk music also incurs other 'aggressive' textures such
as low distorted guitars or Industrial sounds.

**Did you try to tie the music in with each of the specific
levels and scenes after seeing them or did you already
have something in mind before you even saw any of the
game?**
Each Chapter in story mode has unique themes for Banner
and Hulk gameplay yet some themes are reused with different
orchestrations.

The inspiration for the music came from both the look of the
game and the game play. I often spoke with the game designers about the 'scenes' they were directing and tried to com-
pose music within the established chapter themes that
worked interactively with the action. I designed an interactive
music engine to author these music cues to game events.

What is your favorite piece in the game?
Banner music: "Sleeping Gamma Dogs Never Lie"

Hulk Music: "HulkAtraz"

What is your favorite type of music?
It varies. As a saxophonist I love Jazz. But right now, music
that successfully combines different varied ethnic styles is
very exciting to me and I don't mean new age looped fodder
like 'Deep Forest'. I just saw a concert of a group of Tuvan
Throat singer / instrumentalists called 'Huun Huur Tuur' and
they were amazing; imagine Tibetan Monks doing Hank
Williams covers. Very virtuostic playing and singing. I can't
wait to work on a game where I can hire these guys! (Who
am I kidding?)

What was your favorite aspect about this project?
Composing the interactive music and designing the tools for
it.

**After completing the game, what do you expect/want
people to say about their gaming experience?**
I would like them to say that they felt as if they were actually
in the game as they played.

What are you most proud of concerning the game?
The game team. It has been the best production experience I
have ever had. We all really came together in the crunch.

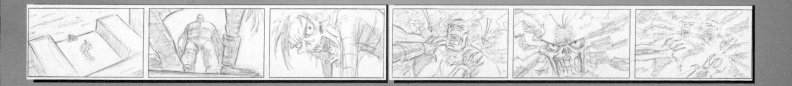

BRYAN BRANDT

Hobbies
Reading comics, rolling dice.

Major Titles Worked On
None

Favorite Food to Snack on While Gaming
Tomato soup.

Favorite Movie
Blade II. It's all about the elbow drop.

Most Recent Gaming Obsession
Soul Calibur 2, Devil May Cry 2

What role did you play in the Hulk project? Or, what did your specific day-to-day tasks include?
I was the fight and animation programmer, but we all end up having to wear multiple hats around here.

Upon discovering that Radical was asked to develop The Hulk, what was your immediate "gut reaction" about being given the opportunity?
I just hoped Hulk would be able to punch a lot. Luckily, as it turns out, he does.

Trying to incorporate the designers' ideas and plan into a fully playable–and enjoyable–game sounds incredibly difficult. How do you even begin? What's the process?
What's great about this job is you end up having to deal with so many different disciplines just to get a single aspect of the game tuned to completion.

For any given combat move, it's an iterative process: First, the designers come up with an attack that they'd like Hulk to perform. The animators whip up a rudimentary animation of the attack. The designers take the animation and then script it to be triggered appropriately in the game, and play with its timings until it "feels" good. Once that's finalized, the animators go back and make it look pretty. Even after that, the effects and audio guys go in and add sound and particle effects to complete the move.

I'm just there to help the process along, to make sure everything works as it should.

Are there times when you just play through a level or section and say, "That's perfect!" or think of a few new tweaks that would improve it? If so, are there any specific instances that come to mind?
The sight of a pack of Gamma Dogs streaming down the chasm in "Without Ethics" still sends chills down my spine. And there's something deeply satisfying about being able to pick up a soldier and watching him bounce off the helicopter you just threw him at.

What sequence, level or element are you most proud of? Did a particular sequence or special move not make it into the build? If so, why?
I'm definitely most proud of Hulk's combat abilities in the game. The designers and animators did a great job of filling out his motion tree with all kinds of whacky charges, combos and throws, all while staying true to the character.

As for stuff that got cut, we originally had a much more complex grappling system designed for grabs between Hulk and large characters. It ultimately was dropped because it slowed gameplay down, and wouldn't have been appropriate without a lot more work.

What was the trickiest task given to you and how did you solve it?
Keeping the designers and animators happy. Unfortunately, it can't be solved.

What was your favorite aspect about this project?
The team, because they are the most talented and passionate bunch of people I've ever worked with, and because we successfully refrained from killing each other along the way.

After completing the game, what do you expect/want people to say about their gaming experience?
I just hope people have a good time smacking dudes around as the ever-lovin' Hulk.

What are you most proud of concerning the game?
Punch, gamma, action against a soldier. Try it, you'll like it.

GAMMA SOLDIER

ROBOT

FLUX

BRYAN GILLINGHAM — LEAD CHARACTER ANIMATOR

Hobbies
Video games, Board games, Basketball, Comic Books, Drawing

Major Titles Worked On
Hulk is my first major title

Favorite Food to Snack on While Gaming
Nachos and Salsa, Beer

Favorite Movie
Aliens, Drunken Master, Lord of the Rings, The Matrix, Ninja Scroll, Sanjuro, Yojimbo, the list goes on...

Most Recent Gaming Obsession
Soul Calibur 2, Golden Sun 2, Settlers of Catan

What role did you play in the Hulk project? Or, what did your specific day-to-day tasks include?
Lead Animator. First and foremost, my day to day job was to animate. I was also in charge of maintaining the focus of the animation team, making sure the style and design of the content was on track. My job also included making sure the content fits well according to the overall design, and keeping tabs on where and when these animations are used.

Upon discovering that Radical was asked to develop The Hulk, what was your immediate "gut reaction" about being given the opportunity?

I'm a big Marvel Universe fan, and hearing that we had a chance to work on a comic book licence got me really excited.

The characters look great. How did you achieve their likenesses?
We've taken a lot of reference from comic books, live action and various game titles that dealt with the scale of characters we have on the Hulk game. We've had to factor in the bulk and size of the Hulk, while not hindering the overall speeds of the gameplay. I really wanted to achieve those classic comic book style dynamic extreme poses, with quick powerful motions. I'm fairly happy with what we've achieved for the Hulk and the Boss characters.

Do you have a character that you couldn't wait to work on? If so, who was it and why?
Since pre-production, I've always had fun working on the Hulk's animations. It was a pleasure to work on a character of his size and proportions. Making him move like a great big force of nature was the overall idea. It was really satisfying animating his trademarked "sonic clap", or gamma punch moves, and seeing that being used in the game. With the

Hulk, achieving those classic comic book poses weren't really difficult, it seemed to come naturally. He was definitely the most fun of all the characters to work with.

Was there a particular special move that was difficult to incorporate?
I would say the most difficult move to deal with was Hulk's jump. It was one of those things that we needed to be really aware of when deciding on the final height and distance the Hulk would travel in. When designing something like a "jump" for a character, you really need to factor how it would interact with the other parts of the game. From level design to camera work, travel speed to collision volumes, all of these aspects would be primarily effected and compromised if done without a great deal of planning and foresight.

The Hulk is one of the most recognizable comic book licenses and the characters are household names. What were a few characteristics that you wanted to capture in the game?
We took reference from the comic books primarily, in creating the moves of the Hulk and the Boss characters. Achieving really strong poses, and powerful dynamic motions was basically our main goal. Plus, we wanted to make Hulk look really angry.

What was your favorite aspect about this project?
I have two. The first was seeing the animations that we've created, working and interacting within the game. It's really satisfying to see that little part of the project you've dealt with, being integrated into the "larger world" of our project. Also hearing the buzz within the team room of "Wow, that move is cool!", and "Sweet! He can do that!?", can really give you instant payoff and recognition of one's hard work.

The second aspect is working with this team. I've had a lot of fun developing the game with these guys, working side by side a bunch of really talented and passionate people has been a real comfortable and creative experience. We had good chemistry and communication. During the darker times of the project you'd notice this team has kept it together and has kept our focus. We've got a really good group here...

After completing the game, what do you expect/want people to say about their gaming experience?
HULK SMASH!

ERIC HOLMES

Hobbies
Playing every videogame on every platform, comics, playing videogames, movies, snowboarding, videogames.

Major Titles Worked On
State of Emergency, Sled Storm (PS2), THE HULK!

Favorite Food to Snack on While Gaming
Irn Bru.

Favorite Movie
Blade Runner, Once Upon A Time In The West, Fight Club, Rashomon

After staring at the big green guy every for the past year and a half I'm sure that buying a ticket to Hulk and watching that movie is going to be one incredible experience.

Most Recent Gaming Obsession
Tekken 4

Upon discovering that Radical was asked to develop The Hulk, what was your immediate "gut reaction" about being given the opportunity?
It was like a cross between a surge of adrenaline and Christmas combined. The chance to contribute to THE HULK is a great opportunity and a huge responsibility. The fact that I was helping shape THE HULK game and a part of 2003's movie phenomenon kept my motivation at peak throughout. It's a cliché, but it's also true—Hulk was a dream project.

What one element were you most excited to get your hands on and begin designing?
Designing and building the character functionality; getting Hulk running around and doing things on demand. Hulk can perform many amazing feats that only Hulk can do—and that players expect to be able to do in a Hulk game. You have a hero that promises many abilities, but you have to carefully manage people's expectations.

The challenge of mapping all those fantastic powers onto a gamepad and start feeling what it was like to BE the Hulk was a demanding but fun task. Once you've got that foundation complete it is much easier for the rest of the game structure to come into place.

Throughout the process, you inevitably saw continual improvements. When did the game truly begin capturing the feel and look that you wanted to achieve?
Balancing the difficulty was one of our major obstacles. Hulk is a character that is inherently tough, so we had to have a legion of enemies we could throw at him and keep reinforcing them.

What's your favorite level? Why?
I have a couple of favorites—I love "Inner Torment" because it's a great Hulk sandbox straight away from pressing 'start'. It's just plain fun.

The rooftops are a complete rollercoaster ride of a level and deliver something that people expect; epic Hulk jumps and over the top combat.

Our Chapter 3 military base was also a lot of fun because it

brings the player right into the movie experience.

The boss levels are great fun because of the individual personalities and abilities of each boss. Flux's voice is a hoot.

What was your favorite aspect about this project?
Difficult question. The game itself was crying out to be made—who wouldn't want to go on a rampage as HULK? This made it really easy to be passionate about it. We had great 'behind the scenes' access with the Universal Theatrical movie production, thanks to our publisher, Universal Interactive. It was inspiring to see what the movie team was creating. Finally, this is a great team full of fantastic people. To be surrounded by so much talent and enthusiasm made it easy to put in all the extra work that's made the HULK game what it is today.

The licensing of this project was sure to include a few interesting restrictions to which you had to adhere, can you mention one or two?
Our project was secretive—it was really hard not to tell everyone I know that I was working on this game and about all the great stuff we were making. The dream project—and I couldn't share it with anyone!

This game is being released simultaneously on three consoles. What were some of the issues that arose concerning this situation?
Finding a combination of controls that would work and work WELL on all styles of gamepad was a challenge. The low-level stuff was not a problem for me—thankfully Radical has great foundation technology which allows us to develop on all three consoles simultaneously, while invisibly taking advantage of what each console's hardware does best.

What was the trickiest task given to you and how did you solve it?
Giving a destructible world that didn't just let the player go anywhere, because obviously you have to reach some objective or another. Hulk is so powerful that you can't just use the regular language of videogames to restrict him. Flames don't hurt him, locked doors can't stop him, he can break through most walls, huge drops mean nothing to a character who can jump for miles, there are no enemies who are truly stronger than he is. Designing a game around this is something of a conundrum, as you want the player to feel like THE HULK, but you don't want to damage the core experience; that feeling of being a cat among the pigeons.

We developed a language of environmental structure, developed our own language to show the player what he can destroy versus damage. We also use the camera as a way of nudging the player in the right direction.

What was it like working with the Bruce Banner of the movie, Eric Bana?
Eric was a big boost to our game. Eric worked with us during the movie production meaning the Bruce Banner you get in the game is really close to the Bruce Banner you're going to see in the movie. Eric is a talented professional and our game really benefits from his contribution.

After completing the game, what do you expect/want people to say about their gaming experience?
"If the Leader's head is that big, how can his neck support it?"

What are you most proud of concerning the game as a whole?
The feeling you get when you hold that gamepad in your hand.

When you see someone start the very first level and they begin playing the game, they have a GREAT BIG SMILE on their face. They FEEL like the HULK and they have FUN!

Through hard work we've brought the experience of being the savage HULK onto a bunch of buttons and a couple of sticks; it's immediate but has depth, it's fun with a level of challenge. When you see people get a kick out of playing the game you know your team has brought it together and done something right.

CHRIS CUDAHY

LEAD PROGRAMMER

Hobbies
I haven't had very much spare time lately! When I do though, I enjoy juggling, gaming and random construction projects (building a telescope at the moment).

Major Titles Worked On
The Hulk is my first major title.

Favorite Food to Snack on While Gaming
Pizza. The local delivery place sends me love letters.

Most Recent Gaming Obsession
I've been playing EverQuest lately, with some breaks for a couple RTS's and some retro gaming.

What role did you play in the Hulk project? Or, what did your specific day-to-day tasks include?
My title is Lead Programmer. This involves setting up the architecture so that all the modules that go into The Hulk can talk to each other, providing support to other programmers on the team and adding in other functionality as we need it.

Upon discovering that Radical was asked to develop The Hulk, what was your immediate "gut reaction" about being given the opportunity?
I was excited about doing the Hulk. It's a character that fits into a game very well. He's big, green, instantly recognizable and everyone knows that he's going to be smashing everything. Of course the details of all that are a lot of work!

All of the builds during the process must complicate things as new bugs are discovered. How do you keep track of them all and what's the process for eliminating them?
We keep a database of all the bugs that are found. This has information about how to reproduce the problem, what build and platform it occurred on and who found the bug. After they are reported they are triaged and assigned to the person who can fix the problem most efficiently. Everyone on the Hulk team did an amazing job of keeping on top things, and the QA team did a huge amount of work to track down all the bugs.

Keeping an eye on the bug list and the deadline at the same time would drive most people crazy. How'd you keep your sanity?
Just chugging away at the list. We kept the bugs in a priority list and did the most important ones as early as possible. Doing that meant that we had a reasonable idea of how long it would take to fix everything and wouldn't get stuck at the end with a lot of crazy hard to fix bugs.

What sequence, level or element are you most proud of? Did a particular sequence or special move not make it into the build? If so, why?
After you've been fighting in an area for a while and the place is covered with damage decals and broken props it just looks completely trashed. Doing a fully charged up rage slam in a crowd of soldiers and props is a good moment as well, everything explodes and flies up in the air.

What was the trickiest task given to you and how did you solve it?
Got to be the memory card support. Each console manufacturer has a very specific set of rules to follow, and such as what to do with a full memory card or when someone puts in one that's broken. Some of the rules for one platform contradict the ones for another platform. So the logic for handling everything that can happen gets quite convoluted. Fortunately I had a couple of great people working with me on this.

What was your favorite aspect of this project?
Somewhere after alpha when we had most of the code features in and the designers were tuning the gameplay and the levels. I was playing the game to test out some new code and I suddenly realized that it was a fun game to play! Everything came together rapidly and it was very exciting.

After completing the game, what do you expect/want people to say about their gaming experience?
I'd like them to come away from the game and say that they felt like they were the Hulk, and had fun playing him. My favorite reaction so far has been my wife doing rage slams and running around growling "Rawrrrrr!"

TIM BENNISON

Hobbies
Playing console games, SF movies and novels, driving my 99 Firebird Formula, watercolor painting

Major Titles Worked On
Simpsons Road Rage, Dark Summit, MTV Snowboarding, Independence Day, Powerplay 98, Jackie Chan Stuntmaster

Favorite Food to Snack on While Gaming
Protein Bars, Protein Shakes, anything with protein

Favorite Movie
Star Wars Episode 4

Most Recent Gaming Obsession
Vice City

What role did you play in the Hulk project? Or, what did your specific day-to-day tasks include?
I was the Producer (which basically means you get the worst computer setup and your game build times take 3 hours)

While not waiting for game builds to complete, in my spare time, I managed everyone on the team, helped set the design and art vision, set up the schedule and made sure we delivered our milestones, gave feedback to everyone about every aspect of the game, played the game for thousands of hours, helped optimize the frame rate, closed about 6,000 bugs and ordered meals for the team.

Upon discovering that Radical was asked to develop The Hulk, what was your immediate "gut reaction" about being given the opportunity?
Oh my god! This is going to be the coolest project of all time!

Managing a project of this magnitude seems like an incredible task. What's your secret?
Aside from the obvious stimulants such as caffeine, you've got to rely on the talent of your team (and we have plenty of that).

How do you keep your teams focused and motivated during the stressful stretches of the project that were sure to be time consuming?
We had a saying: "Do it for the kids!", meaning that this is all about creating a fun experience for the player, this kept us focused. For motivation, we knew that The Hulk was a golden opportunity both in terms of the gameplay potential of the character and the crossover potential of ideas and visuals from the movie.

With so many different aspects of a game being worked on simultaneously, what priorities need to be set in order to maintain a timely schedule? Is there a specific process that would cause everything else to stop if it wasn't on schedule?
It's a complex web of processes that all interact together. You've got to keep the technical, art, sound and game design aspects all moving forward at the same time. You've got to be on the lookout constantly for snags and bottlenecks in any of these areas. Game design is the root of everything; technical requirements, artistic direction, sound direction all stem from the creative inspiration of the design.

Are there ever issues with having developed "perfect" elements of a game that simply can't be integrated? For example, would the situation occur where an incredible piece of music and a gorgeous cinematic simply didn't work well together?
We were fortunate in the sense that a lot of elements DID come together in the making of this game. A lot of our problems came about when we got too ambitious, we had levels and characters almost completed that had to be cut, we had features such as combat with helicopter gunships that we didn't have time to pull off properly, so we cut the feature. This happens in every production, but it's always tough to cut things.

What was your favorite aspect about this project?
There was a moment when enough stuff came together and we all started playing the game and realizing that it was actually FUN; this is the best moment in any game production. After 14 months of slaving away, you get to play the game as it was meant to be played, and you start to see the fun emerge.

After completing the game, what do you expect/want people to say about their gaming experience?
I'd like people to get a real adrenaline rush playing with the power of the Hulk. Hopefully, people will agree that we delivered a unique combination of gameplay and story which respects both the Marvel Hulk universe and the movie Hulk universe.

What was the trickiest task given to you and how did you solve it?
There were a lot of tricky tasks, too many to count. One task that comes to mind is trying to integrate hand-to-hand combat, physically-simulated weapon interaction, and animation into one package that is easy to use and fun.

What are you most proud of concerning the game?
I believe that we delivered on our goal: you get to be the HULK, that's very cool.

LINDZ WILLIAMSON

Hobbies
Secret Geek hobby: Collecting comics – Ultimate Xmen, Uncanny, Xmen, Xiles, Powers, Battlechasers, Crimson, The Authority

Normal hobbies: cooking, mountain biking, reading, travelling

Major Titles Worked On
None that I can speak of at the moment, all my previous games never existed in the real world. Hulk is my first real project that lived to meet the public.

Favorite Food to Snack on While Gaming
A mix of Jalapeño Jack & English toffee popcorn, it's the perfect salty sweet combo.

Favorite Movie
You know, I really hate this question. There are so many great movies that I hate narrowing it down to one. Although I am really excited to see a lot of movies this summer and the Hulk is definitely at the top of the list.

Most Recent Gaming Obsession
I haven't played a lot of games in the last six months as all my waking hours have been spent on the Hulk. I'm way behind on playing any of the recent titles. I still need to finish Two Towers and Buffy on Xbox. But I'm looking forward to playing Soul Calibur 2, it looks so nice on the Gamecube and I really enjoyed the original on the Dreamcast.

What role did you play in the Hulk project? Or, what did your specific day-to-day tasks include?
I'm the Project Manager so I basically plan out who does what and when. Which really means I spend a lot of time running around asking people to do stuff and then bugging them to get it done.

Upon discovering that Radical was asked to develop The Hulk, what was your immediate "gut reaction" about being given the opportunity?
I think I actually said, "OMG we get to do a Marvel license, that is so cool!" I grew up watching the TV show and I'm a total Marvel fan. The Hulk is just such a huge piece of pop culture and for me there couldn't be a better license to work on.

What was your favorite aspect about this project?
So many things went so well that it's hard to narrow down. I'm really proud of everything thing that the Hairclub team has achieved. Everyone worked so hard for such a long time and we all agonized over every decision and detail. I'm just happy that it all came together so well and above all that the game is FUN.

After completing the game, what do you expect/want people to say about their gaming experience?
I really just want people to have fun with it.

What are you most proud of concerning the game?
I am so proud of the whole game. I love the way the game looks with the cell shading and how it plays. My favorite level is Betrayal, as I never get tired of chucking guys off buildings and I love fighting the Robots in the military base.

There are many industries that require a person with your talents. What is it about the gaming industry that pulled you in and keeps you here?
The gaming industry is so diverse. The people I work with every day are the smartest, most talented and dedicated people I've ever known. Since it's such a young industry people come from all over the world to work on a game and have various different backgrounds and experiences. Making games is hard, don't let anyone fool you into thinking it's easy, but when you get all these crazy, smart, talented people together under one roof you can't help but have a good time.

JONATHAN LIM

Hobbies
Games, movies, basketball (Go Suns!) and various other sports, reading, the usual.

Major Titles Worked On
Simpsons Road Rage, Monsters Inc. Scream Arena, and, of course, The Hulk

Favorite Food to Snack on While Gaming
Popcorn! Mmm, buttery goodness

Favorite Movie
Top Gun. I cannot count the times I've seen this movie growing up.

Most Recent Gaming Obsession
Legend of Zelda: The Wind Waker, phenomenal

What role did you play in the Hulk project? Or, what did your specific day-to-day tasks include?
I was the test lead on this massive project and that included a wide variety of things to do. Generally I coordinate the other testers around me as well as test myself, and work closely with the project manager and the Lead designer to make sure that the game stays true to their vision

Upon discovering that Radical was asked to develop The Hulk, what was your immediate "gut reaction" about being given the opportunity?
Wow! It was a great chance for Radical to really make a name for itself and I was excited to be able to be a part of this great game.

What was your favorite aspect about this project?
Working with the team has been an absolute blast. We have a great team that gets along and it shows. Despite all the hours we had to work, it was fun day in and day out because the team kept it light and fun.

After completing the game, what do you expect/want people to say about their gaming experience?
I hope people enjoy the sheer destructibility in this game and the myriad of moves that the Hulk has available to him. Most of all, I hope that it was way beyond their expectations for a game based on a movie.

What are you most proud of concerning the game?
I am proud of how the team really pulled together and made such a wonderful game. There were some rough times but when it mattered, we delivered something that is fun and wildly entertaining.

There are many industries that require a person with your talents. What is it about the gaming industry that pulled you in and keeps you here?
What can I say? I love games! The majority of the people who work in this industry do so because of the passion they have for games and gaming and I am no different.

LEADER

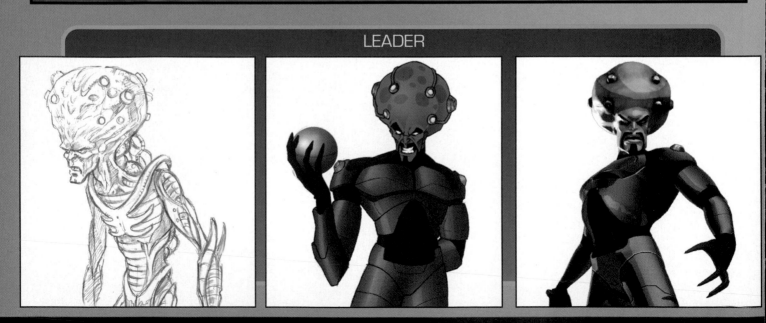

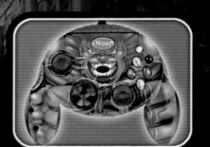

THANK YOUS

BradyGames would like to thank everyone at Universal Interactive who helped with the completion of this guide, especially Craig Howe, John Choon and Michael Scharnikow. We would also like to thank the entire team at Radical for their assistance with this guide, especially Eric Holmes, Tim Bennison, and Bill King.

BRADYGAMES STAFF

PUBLISHER
David Waybright

EDITOR-IN-CHIEF
H. Leigh Davis

MARKETING MANAGER
Janet Eshenour

CREATIVE DIRECTOR
Robin Lasek

LICENSING MANAGER
Mike Degler

ASSISTANT MARKETING MANAGER
Susie Nieman

CREDITS

SENIOR PROJECT EDITOR
Ken Schmidt

BOOK DESIGNER
Dan Caparo

POSTER & COVER DESIGNER
Chris Luckenbill

PRODUCTION DESIGNER
Bob Klunder